THE DOBERMAN PINSCHER

Janice Biniok

The Doberman Pinscher

Project Team
Editor: Mary E. Grangeia
Copy Editor: Joann Woy
Indexer: Elizabeth Walker
Designer: Stephanie Krautheim
Series Design: Stephanie Krautheim and Mada Design
Series Originator: Dominique De Vito

TFH Publications®
President/CEO: Glen S. Axelrod
Executive Vice President: Mark E. Johnson
Publisher: Christopher T. Reggio
Production Manager: Kathy Bontz

TFH Publications, Inc.®
One TFH Plaza
Third and Union Avenues
Neptune City, NJ 07753

Printed and bound in China
11 12 13 14 15   5 7 9 8 6 4

Library of Congress Cataloging-in-Publication Data
Biniok, Janice.
  The doberman pinscher / Janice Biniok.
     p. cm.
  Includes index.
  ISBN 978-0-7938-3688-8 (alk. paper)
  1. Doberman pinscher. I. Title.
  SF429.D6B56 2009
  636.73'6--dc22
                                    2009004283

This book has been published with the intent to provide accurate and authoritative information in regard to the subject matter within. While every reasonable precaution has been taken in preparation of this book, the author and publisher expressly disclaim responsibility for any errors, omissions, or adverse effects arising from the use or application of the information contained herein. The techniques and suggestions are used at the reader's discretion and are not to be considered a substitute for veterinary care. If you suspect a medical problem consult your veterinarian.

Note: In the interest of concise writing, "he" is used when referring to puppies and dogs unless the text is specifically referring to females or males. "She" is used when referring to people. However, the information contained herein is equally applicable to both sexes.

The Leader In Responsible Animal Care For Over 50 Years! ®
www.tfh.com

TABLE OF CONTENTS

HISTORY

of the Doberman Pinscher

Whether you have already purchased your Doberman Pinscher or are thinking about getting one, you have been attracted to this marvelous breed for one reason or another. It is difficult not to admire the Doberman's impressive stature, physical elegance, or the impeccable devotion he has for his master. But this is a complex creature who possesses many qualities, some of which are not so blatantly obvious. By exploring the Doberman's roots, you will truly appreciate who this dog is and how he came to be.

In existence for slightly more than a hundred years, the Doberman Pinscher is considered a newcomer to the world of purebred dogs. However, some of the breeds used in his development, such as the Rottweiler and Greyhound, have been around for many centuries. The Rottweiler was a guardian and protector as far back as Roman times, and the Greyhound can easily be traced to ancient Egypt as far back as 4,000 years ago. There is speculation that the modern Doberman also carries genes from the Weimaraner, German Shorthaired Pointer, Manchester Terrier, and an early form of German Shepherd (also called German Sheepdogs, which are now extinct).

THE DOBERMAN'S GERMAN HERITAGE

How did this unique combination of genes result in the magnificently sleek and impressively powerful animal we see today? In the late 1800s, it was the dream of Herr Karl Louis Dobermann of Apolda, in the province of Thuringia, Germany, to create a superior canine guardian. As a tax collector, personal protection was a priority for him, and as a dog fancier and night watchman for the Public Dog Shelter of Apolda, he had access to a large and varied canine gene pool from which to experiment.

In the process of developing a dog with boldness, agility, bravery, alertness, and intelligence, Louis Dobermann also sought a pleasing appearance after his own fancy. By 1880, he was thoroughly involved in creating what he considered the ideal dog—a large version of a terrier with the same fiery attitude and physical abilities. Hence, the later application of the word "pinscher," a German term for terrier, to describe these dogs. At the

In existence for slightly more than a hundred years, the Doberman Pinscher is considered a newcomer to the world of purebred dogs.

time, however, they were simply known as Dobermann's Dogs.

Louis Dobermann may have been meticulous in his breeding practices, choosing just the right mates to produce his dream dog, but he was not as conscientious in keeping written records. A number of mixed-breeds may have contributed their murky lineage to the present-day Doberman, making it impossible or impractical to keep accurate records of parentage. So, we may never know exactly which breeds and in which proportions they donated their individual qualities.

Louis Dobermann died in 1894, after more than a decade of breeding, and his legacy passed on to Otto Goeller, also from Apolda, Germany. Goeller, owner of von Thuringen Kennels, is not only credited with developing the type of Doberman we see today, but also for promoting interest in the breed. He was responsible for adding the name "Pinscher" to the breed name, and establishing the first Doberman breed club in Germany in 1899, called the National Dobermannpinscher Klub. He also collaborated with other fanciers to develop the first breed standard for the Doberman in 1900. The breed subsequently received official recognition from the German Kennel Club less than a year later.

The production of several dogs around 1896 resulted in what is considered the nucleus of the Doberman breed. The dogs Rambo, Lux, Landgraf, and Schnupp, and the bitches Tilly I, Helmtrude, Hertha, and Elly represented a new strain destined to become the Doberman's founding ancestors. Although these dogs did not

resemble the Doberman as we know him today, having a heavier body and longer hair, their prepotency perpetuated a number of desirable traits.

One of these traits was a protective nature to help them fulfill their purpose as guardians. Another was the courage with which Louis Dobermann wanted them to perform their duties. Initially, temperament was of the utmost importance because these were working dogs developed for a specific purpose. A litter produced by Schnupp was later described by noted historian Horowitz as "deplorable to look at and very ferocious." Lux was also known to have an extremely aggressive nature, and these early dogs quickly earned the Doberman a fearsome reputation that has endured to the present day.

Looks were important not only to please the eye of the beholder, but also to help the dog fulfill his purpose. Adequate size was necessary to give the dog strength and substance. A lean build would make him athletic and agile. And, of course, the dog needed to be well balanced and in good proportion to meet the physical requirements of his job. Ears were cropped to give a sharp, intimidating presence, and at some point in the Doberman's early development, some dogs were born with bobbed tails. This genetic mutation gained much admiration and may have inspired the docking of Doberman tails—a practice still followed today and which contributes to the Doberman's bold image.

The Doberman's coarse appearance was later refined by Louis Dobermann's successors. In addition to the work of Otto Goeller, Goswin Tischler was also instrumental in developing the sleek and attractive animal we now call the Doberman Pinscher. Tischler, owner of the von Groenland Kennels in Apolda, Germany, produced the breed's first champion, Prinz Mitzi von Groenland, in 1895. He is also credited with advancing the development of the Doberman with the production of his famous "five-star litter." The combination of Lux and Tilly I begat five exceptional dogs who were much admired by fanciers of the time. Out of the five dogs— Belling, Greif, Krone, Lottchen, and Tilly II—Belling was the first to be registered in the National Doberman Pinscher Stud Book in Germany.

THE DOBERMAN IN EUROPE

By the early 1900s, the Doberman Pinscher had found his way

Evolution of the Doberman

1880 to 1900: The Doberman had a blunter nose, longer hair, and a slightly stockier build. Some were produced with light-colored eyes, and a few inherited a genetic mutation that resulted in a naturally bobbed tail. An extremely sharp temperament was highly valued.

1900 to 1920: The breed continued to evolve with the introduction of genes from the Greyhound and Manchester Terrier to establish color and coat type, as well as to refine the Doberman's build with a lengthier nose and wiry body. Dobermans of this time were smaller than their modern counterparts and much more terrier-like in appearance.

1920 to 1940: The physical traits of the Doberman became well established and survive to the present day. Breeders began to focus on producing a less aggressive, more stable temperament without sacrificing protectiveness, intelligence, trainability, or loyalty.

Although the roots of the breed are uncertain, it is believed that the Doberman Pinscher originated in Germany around 1900, taking its name from tax collector Louis Dobermann, who developed the breed.

to a number of European countries, including Switzerland, Holland, France, Italy, and Austria. The breed became known to many other countries during World War I (1914 to 1918), when the world was exposed to Germany's military dogs, which included many Doberman Pinschers.

Conditions in Europe during the war were very difficult, with food shortages and starvation gripping much of the continent. Many dogs were put to death because people could no longer afford to feed or care for them. The effects were devastating on Doberman breeding kennels of the time. Philipp Gruenig, a prominent Doberman breeder in Germany, related that 20 of his best breeding stock died of starvation or had to be put down.

If it weren't for Germany's need for Dobermans in military service, and the efforts of German breeders who exported many of their prized stock to save them from the effects of war, the Doberman's continued existence may have been severely compromised. Exportation put all but a few of Germany's top Doberman breeding stock in the hands of foreign countries, including the United States. It was a sacrifice that not only saved the best German breeding stock from vanishing, but also helped distribute the Doberman throughout the world.

World War II (1939 to 1945) also challenged the survival of the Doberman in Germany. Many breeders were once again forced to relinquish their Dobermans for military service. In addition, all dog training and breed clubs were required to be a part of a national organization controlled by the Nazi government. The exportation of dogs was halted, which severely limited the resources of German breeders. Fortunately, enough of the original German bloodlines were preserved to maintain Germany's status as a producer of fine-quality Dobermans after the war.

THE DOBERMAN IN GREAT BRITAIN

Great Britain was already employing dogs for police work and limited military duties during World War I, but it wasn't until after World War II that the Doberman gained a foothold there. It's hard to say why—as the breed's popularity blossomed throughout Europe and the United States—it did not seem to catch on as quickly in Great Britain. Only a dozen or so dogs had been imported to England prior to World War II.

Even as their allies employed Dobermans in the fight against Nazi Germany, the breed was relatively unknown in Great Britain until after the war. Then, in 1948, a Doberman club was formed, primarily through the efforts of Mr. and Mrs. Curnow, who sought to establish the breed in England. In Great Britain, as well as elsewhere in Europe, the breed name was shortened to "Dobermann," since the term "pinscher" (terrier) did not accurately describe the breed. Dobermans have since found a favored following throughout Great Britain.

THE DOBERMAN IN THE UNITED STATES

Doberman Pinschers began to arrive in the United States in the early 1900s. The first registration with the American Kennel Club (AKC) was Doberman Intelectus in 1908. Somewhere along the way, the second "n" in Dobermann was dropped, probably the result of Americans' habit of Americanizing foreign names. But the Doberman still remained an obscure breed to the American general public until after World War I.

The Doberman Pinscher Club of America (DPCA) was founded in 1921 and adopted the official German standard for the breed. American breeders finally had a source of support and guidance. Initially, most breeding stock in the United States was imported from Holland, where the breed had already established firm roots. Eventually, imported dogs began to arrive from other parts of the world, including Germany, the Netherlands, and Russia, making the American Doberman a product of international bloodlines.

By the time World War II began, the United States had already experienced the effectiveness of Germany's war dogs during World War I, and the US Marines convinced their leaders of the need for war dogs of their own. The Doberman became the Marines' dog of choice, and a training facility was established at Camp LeJeune, North Carolina. Working with the DPCA, and assisted by the civilian organization Dogs for Defense, the Marines recruited Dobermans to fill the majority of their dog and handler ranks, aptly calling their dogs "Devil Dogs." This resulted in a population boom

A Breed by Many Names

The Doberman Pinscher has been known by a number of names in different parts of the world throughout the breed's development. Some of the names attributed to the breed include:

Dobermann's Dogs: The early name attributed to dogs bred by Louis Dobermann.

Thuringian Pinschers: The early name for Doberman's Dogs, probably used outside the Thuringia province in Germany to denote the regional origin of the dogs.

Soldatenhunds (Soldier Dogs): A name that may have evolved after the Doberman's use as police or military dogs.

Dobermann Pinscher: The official name adopted when the Doberman was accepted as a new breed in Germany.

Dobermann: The name adopted by Great Britain and some other European countries to disassociate the breed from the Terrier Group.

Doberman Pinscher: The name adopted in the United States, an Americanized form of the German name.

Because most early Dobermans exhibited the typical black and rust color pattern, this became a physical requirement in the original German breed standard. Even though black was a desired color, it quickly became evident that other colors resulted from the mating of black to black Dobermans. Reds (also called brown or liver) and blues gained such favor with fanciers that the breed standard was changed in 1901 to include them. Fawns (also called Isabella) were also in existence since the early 1900s but were not added to the breed standard until 1969.

for the Doberman, with more than 1,000 registrations per year by 1934. By 1941, the Doberman had become the 15th most popular purebred dog in the United States according to AKC registration statistics.

Despite the Doberman's heroic service to this country, and perhaps partly because of it, he was still considered a dog of unsavory repute. The first Doberman to win a Best in Show award at the prestigious Westminster Kennel Club show in New York was Ch. Ferry v. Rauhfelsen in 1939. This dog purportedly achieved his honor without ever being physically examined by the judge. The Doberman name had become synonymous with uncontrollable aggression, and even a dog show judge had enough common sense not to lay a hand on one!

Breeders in the United States had already begun to focus on the Doberman's reliability, intelligence, and loyalty. Without subduing the breed's natural protectiveness, they were establishing a dog with remarkably sound judgment who was trustworthy with children, easy to train, and loyal to the ends of the earth. American-bred dogs are still considered more docile than dogs produced by some European lines. But this new image was not powerful enough to erase stereotypes of the past or to combat the wicked reputation refueled by a number of popular movies produced in the 1970s.

When David Chudnow's film, *The Doberman Gang*, was released in 1972, it relied on the Doberman's reputation for viciousness to create a suspenseful, attention-grabbing plot. Subsequent movies, *The Daring Dobermans*, released in 1973, and *The Amazing Dobermans*, released in 1976, also garnered appeal by casting the Doberman's intimidating physical presence in aggressive roles. Besides preserving a reputation that might have been outgrown, the success of these films had another detrimental effect on the breed.

The popularity of Doberman Pinschers rose dramatically, an effect similar to the rise in popularity of Dalmatians each time Disney releases a new version of its well-known classic, *101 Dalmatians*. As anyone in the business of breeding dogs knows, popularity is not always a good thing. It encourages indiscriminate breeding by those interested only in the financial aspects of meeting an economic demand. This leads to a rise in both physical and temperament faults within a breed that sometimes take decades to bring under control.

The Doberman suddenly found himself second only to the

Poodle in the number of AKC registrations, and concern for the welfare of the breed inspired the formation of the Committee on Population Explosion (COPE) by Judith Fellton in 1976. Clubs and individuals were urged to curtail breeding in order to lessen the popularity of the Doberman and to preserve the quality of the breed. Fortunately, the Doberman has regressed to a more modest placing between 22 and 23 in number of AKC registrations during the last decade, and many of the problems experienced during the breed's heyday of popularity have diminished considerably.

The Doberman Pinscher has evolved considerably since Louis Dobermann's time. The breed has become more refined in appearance and more docile in temperament, making the Doberman more appropriate as a family pet and allowing him to fulfill many other duties besides protection work. Dobermans are employed as search-and-rescue dogs, therapy dogs, guide dogs for the blind, and sport dogs, as well as in many other capacities. This attractive and versatile breed is destined to maintain a respectable rank in popularity, and the fortunate person who owns a Doberman is privileged to enjoy his many talents and admirable qualities.

Along with his talent for protection work, the Doberman is admired for his impressive stature, physical elegance, and impeccable devotion to his master.

2

CHARACTERISTICS
of the Doberman Pinscher

The Doberman's beauty is captivating. His powerful presence is riveting. If you find yourself standing in awe of this marvelous creature, you've joined the ranks of many others who have been drawn to the Doberman's aesthetically pleasing physique. He is sleek, strong, and almost perpetually alert. Attractive color patterns, a size that is neither too big nor too small, and the practicality of a short coat add up to make the Doberman a serious consideration if you seek an easy-care pet, an athletic sport dog partner, or an eye-catching show dog prospect.

But looks are only half the picture. To determine whether a Doberman should be in your future, you must also consider his temperament and specific needs. While certain traits are desired and admired by some, they may cause problems or concerns for others. Finding the dog of your dreams involves an in-depth evaluation of your own wants and needs as well as considering the physical and emotional needs of the dog. If you choose your dog judiciously and responsibly, it can result in a match made in heaven!

PHYSICAL CHARACTERISTICS

Dobermans are unique from any other breed of dog in the world. How did they get this way? What sets them apart from other breeds and makes all Dobermans essentially look the same? Selectively breeding dogs who share similar characteristics eventually produces uniform offspring so that a breed type is created. You might call it "artificial evolution." The Doberman evolved through many years of meticulous, selective breeding.

But breeding is not an exact science. Each dog possesses slight differences in temperament and physical characteristics—no two are exactly the same. In order that these differences do not become so variable that they destroy the sameness that defines a breed, breed standards are created as guidelines to encourage the breeding of dogs who most closely meet the same criteria for personality and appearance. The following traits are the physical requirements for Doberman Pinschers as set forth in the breed standards accepted by the American Kennel Club (AKC) and the Kennel Club (KC).

The Doberman Pinscher Breed Profile

Height	Males: 26 inches (66 cm) to 28 inches (71 cm)
	Females: 24 inches (61 cm) to 26 inches (66 cm)
Weight	Approx. 66 to 88 pounds (30 to 40 kg)
Life Expectancy	10 to 12 years
Coat Color	Black, red (brown), blue, and fawn (Isabella) with rust markings on chest, throat, muzzle, above the eyes, under the tail, and on all legs and feet
Hypoallergenic	No
Shedding	Moderate shedder with short, stiff hair
Grooming	Weekly brushing, twice per week during shedding season
Drooling	None
Minimum Accommodations	Does best in a home with a yard
Energy Level	Moderate to high
Exercise Time	30 minutes twice per day
Trainability	Learns quickly
Protectiveness	Moderate to high

General Appearance

The Doberman Pinscher is a sleek but powerful dog. He is well muscled for strength and yet lean enough for agility and speed. This dog is bred to be an athlete! He has a well tucked up belly modeled after the speedy sight hounds and the strong, wide loins and broad hips of a working dog. His ribs are well sprung to make plenty of room for the energy-producing lungs and heart, and his back is short and straight to help provide powerful forward movement and flexibility in maneuvers. He is truly a powerhouse.

The Doberman's general appearance is one that commands respect. He carries his head proudly atop an elegantly arched neck, and his bold, square stance clearly represents his coordination and balance. He holds his tail in a reserved position no higher than a slight elevation from the body, which is a noble tail carriage neither too high nor too low. Any other posture might undermine the Doberman's quality of fearlessness and determination.

Well put together, the Doberman's temperament and physical traits combine to create an air of pride and nobility. He is watchful and courageous, as well as loyal and obedient. There is no better composition for a dog intended for personal protection. His beauty and grace add even more chocolate to the pudding. It is a rare person who does not gain a little self-esteem by possessing a Doberman.

Size

Both the AKC and the KC specify ideal heights of 27.5 inches (69 cm) for males and 25.5 inches (65 cm) for females. These sizes do not allow much variation in the breed because size is one of the characteristics that make the Doberman unique. Resembling a large pinscher, they have to be big enough to package the strength they need as guard dogs, but they also need to be small enough to retain the quickness of a terrier. If they were any smaller, they would lose their powerful and intimidating presence, and if they were any larger, they would become less agile or even clumsy.

Head

The Doberman Pinscher's head mimics the sleek lines of the body. The top of his long, triangular skull widens from the nose to the base of the ears in a smooth, unbroken line, creating an elegantly tapered wedge. The same type of wedge can be viewed from the side, as the full, powerful jaws fill in the widest part.

A square, medium-sized dog, the Doberman Pinscher is agile, muscular, and possesses great endurance and speed.

This head shape allows only a slight stop, which is the drop from the eyes to the bridge of the nose. Flat cheeks support the straight, angular lines of the head.

Such a head does not offer abundant space between the eyes, a characteristic that some believe indicates a lack of intelligence. But the Doberman has completely dispelled the myth that a broad forehead is necessary for superior brain capacity: It is one of the most intelligent breeds of dog in the world.

Ears

The base of the Doberman's ears are set level with the top of his skull, which makes them appear to be sharp, straight projections from the top of the head when they are cropped and gives a slight rise to the base of the ears when they are left uncropped. The AKC breed standard shows a preference for cropped ears, but entertains the possibility of uncropped ears by describing them as normally cropped. The KC, located in a country in which it is illegal to crop ears, prefers the ears to be as small as possible so as not to give the Doberman a hound-like appearance.

Although cropping has become a controversial issue, comparing cropped and uncropped Dobermans does reveal stark differences in the effect of their appearance. Cropped ears are more representative of Louis Dobermann's vision of the perfect guard dog because they give the dog an impression of keen alertness. The angularly

The Doberman has a very sleek coat with short, close-lying hair that is smooth and shiny.

cropped ears are also an attractive compliment to the Doberman's wedge-shaped head. Uncropped dogs, on the other hand, possess floppy ears that give an entirely different impression altogether. They soften the rigid lines of the face, making the Doberman appear much tamer.

Even though show dogs are most often cropped, pet owners do have a choice and should remember that it is strictly a cosmetic procedure—although it does involve some risks. If you do not plan to exhibit your dog, you should research all the pros and cons of cropping to make an educated decision.

Eyes

The Doberman's oval-shaped eyes are consistent with his reputation as a working guard dog—they indicate his seriousness and determination and also reflect his vigorous energy. The color of the eyes is determined by the coat color, but in all cases the irises should be uniform in shade. Black dogs have medium to dark brown eyes; reds, blues, and fawns should have eyes that match the color of their markings.

Mouth

The Doberman's lips are tightly fitted to his muzzle, and the number and placement of his teeth are very specific in the AKC breed standard. This is probably due to the fact that some early ancestors of the breed had problems with missing or misplaced teeth; a flaw that still shows up occasionally in modern Dobermans. The Doberman should have 22 teeth in the lower jaw and 20 in the upper jaw, and they should be set in the appropriate scissors bite, with the top teeth closely overlapping the lower teeth.

The AKC standard does allow for teeth that are slightly overshot or undershot, but there are strict guidelines concerning this. If the teeth are overshot more than 3/16 inch (0.48 cm) or undershot more than 1/8 inch (0.3 cm), the dog is not just penalized, he is disqualified. The KC standard is slightly more forgiving for undershot, overshot, or badly arranged teeth; these flaws are described as simply being undesirable.

Coat and Color

The Doberman has a very sleek coat with short, close-lying hair that is smooth and shiny. When properly groomed, it has

Albino Dobermans

Albinism in Dobermans is a genetic mutation—and therefore a hereditary condition—that causes a lack of pigmentation in the skin, coat, and iris of the eye. An albino Doberman will usually have white fur, pink skin, and blue eyes, although some albinos may exhibit a small degree of shading or coloration. Due to the higher incidence of health problems (and temperament problems) associated with the condition, albino Dobermans are not eligible to be shown and are subject to limited registration with the AKC. Limited registration is used as a means of discouraging the breeding of albinos by making any puppies produced by these dogs ineligible for registration.

Breed standards exist to standardize the characteristics of a breed. Without them, there might exist so many variations within a breed that it would be difficult to distinguish purebreds from nonpurebreds. Standards describe a breed in great detail and outline the physical and temperament traits considered ideal. Although it might be impossible to find a dog who meets all of the requirements perfectly, standards provide a scale by which dogs can be judged. Standards also serve as blueprints for breeders who strive to produce the ideal dog. Dogs who come closest to meeting the requirements in a standard are awarded at dog shows, and this provides the incentives necessary to keep purebred dogs clearly recognizable.

the sheen of freshly polished mahogany. This attractive canine attire comes in a variety of colors: black, red (considered brown in the KC standard), blue, and fawn (a shade of tan also referred to as Isabella). All of these colors are accented with rust-colored markings above the eyes and under the tail, and on the muzzle, throat, chest, legs, and feet. The AKC breed standard does allow for the occasional white patch on the chest as long as it does not exceed 1/2 square inch (1.3 sq cm), but the KC considers any white markings highly undesirable.

Both the AKC and the KC allow an imperceptible undercoat on the neck, which means the hair may be slightly thicker in this area, but it should not be noticeable to the eye. The rest of the body should be covered in a thick, flat coat devoid of waves or undercoat. Hair that forms a ridge along the back of the neck or spine is highly undesirable.

Forequarters and Hindquarters

The forequarters and hindquarters are described in great detail in the breed standards because they have such a great impact on the Doberman's conformation, balance, stance, and movement. The shoulder blade should slant across the base of the neck at a 45-degree angle when the dog is viewed from the side, and it should meet the upper foreleg at a crisp 90-degree angle. The length of the shoulder blade should be equal to the length of the upper foreleg.

The hindquarters should be in balance with the forequarters, with the hipbones slightly lower than the spine to create a gently rounded croup. The upper shank (from hip to knee) is the same length as the lower shank (from knee to hock). The Doberman's thighs should be well muscled and meet the hip squarely at a right angle.

The legs and feet should be straight, without any inward or outward turning of the elbows, toes, or hocks. The elbow must lie close to the side so that it does not impair smooth movement of the leg and shoulder. The pasterns on the front and rear legs should be nearly perpendicular to the ground.

The feet are described as catlike due to the close-fitting, arched toes. Splayed toes or flat feet are highly unattractive in a Doberman and also not as functional. Dewclaws are usually removed since they serve no purpose and can blemish the clean lines of this elegantly constructed canine.

Gait and Movement

Doberman Pinschers with the correct conformation will display balanced movement with a vigorous forward reach from the forequarters and a strong driving stride from the hindquarters. The feet and legs will not flail to the inside or outside when trotting, and the rear will travel in a straight line with the front.

The natural and correct trotting gait for a Doberman involves single-tracking, which means the rear feet hit the ground in the exact same spot as the front feet. This is an unusual trait; most dogs travel with the rear feet landing slightly behind the tracks of the forefeet. The AKC breed standard is slightly confusing on this point because it states that the rear legs move in line with the front legs on the same side, implying the Doberman executes a pacing gait. This is not the case. This description is intended to refer to the movement necessary for single-tracking.

TEMPERAMENT AND REPUTATION

More striking than the physical appearance of the Doberman is his reputation. He easily gives the impression of a dog to be feared. The Doberman's reputation as a vicious, aggressive animal is one that has endured since the inception of the breed. When Louis Dobermann embarked on his endeavor to create the perfect guard dog, this is exactly the impression he desired to create so that the

Early in its development, the Doberman was bred to be a superior canine guardian and companion.

mere sight of the dog would be enough to thwart robbers or intruders. As if the dog's size and powerful build were not enough to intimidate those with less than honorable intentions, the addition of sharply cropped ears and boldly docked tail definitely created an animal with a devilish countenance.

Historical Reputation

Initial breeding stock was chosen for "sharpness," which is aggressiveness. It is true that many of the Doberman's early ancestors were known to be exceptionally aggressive, sometimes unruly, and often described as very

Dobermans make good pets provided that the breed type is a good match for the owner.

ferocious. This reputation has endured to the present day, despite modern breeding practices that produce mentally sound and extremely loyal dogs.

The Doberman's nasty reputation continues to be perpetuated by Hollywood's portrayal of him as a villain dog. Apparently, a black dog with pointed ears and flashing white fangs appears to be made of the same substance as nightmares, but the public never has the opportunity to see what goes on behind the scenes of movie production. The fact that Dobermans can be trained to perform such complex sequences in films is testament to the fact that they are highly intelligent and possess superior trainability.

Protectiveness

The Doberman of today, while fiercely loyal to his family, should not be overly protective or aggressive. In fact, the standard for this breed is one of the few that specifically address the type of temperament the dog should have, and it firmly disqualifies any animal displaying vicious (or shy) behavior. Keeping in mind the Doberman's intended purpose, he should be willing to defend his home and family, but do so using sound judgment.

Most fanciers of the breed would hope that Dobermans with a "hair trigger" (those who are short-tempered, unpredictable, and uncontrollable) have been eliminated from the gene pool by now. But there are still those who engage in irresponsible breeding, and a few who purposely produce vicious dogs to profit from the demand for fierce guard dogs. These bad-apple breeders continue to mar the reputation of the breed and make it imperative to scrutinize the source of a dog carefully prior to purchase.

A stable temperament is not only required for a show dog, it is also required for one intended as a pet. Because the great majority of Dobermans are kept as pets rather than as working dogs, the breed might have become extinct if it continued to have the intimidating temperament that discouraged many people from owning one in the past. Their ongoing popularity shows that the modern Doberman does make a good pet, provided that the breed type is a good match for the owner.

Even so, the Doberman's protective nature is a serious consideration for anyone contemplating owning one. Protectiveness obviously provides some benefits, but it is also a form of liability. You can't berate a dog who is performing his instinctive duty when he growls menacingly at strangers who enter your home unannounced. Your dog may not know that some of your friends or relatives are accustomed to walking right in without knocking first!

On the other hand, nothing can replace the sense of security a Doberman has to offer. In an uncertain and unsafe world, he does provide a priceless measure of confidence. With adequate socialization and training, the Doberman's protective instinct becomes discriminatory and controlled, making him a safe and judicious defender of life and property.

Dobermans are actually very selective. They do not view every stranger as an enemy. You might notice a stark difference in your dog's reaction to the approach of women and children as opposed to the approach of a solitary man (especially if the man is large and intimidating). In fact, a Doberman will often exercise differentiation, which means he may let his guard down when circumstances call for it. He may be perfectly tolerant in allowing all kinds of people to enter and exit your home during a party, but, of course, he would be on full alert if someone tried to enter your home in the middle of the night.

Independence

The Doberman's independent nature is another consideration. Dobermans have their own mind, and they like to use it! This is clearly a valuable trait in a dog required to exercise his own judgment in the course of police work or guard duty, but it can be frustrating if you are not accustomed to handling a dog with this type of mindset. Contrary to popular belief, however, Dobermans are exceptionally easy to train when the right methods are applied.

Formal obedience training is highly recommended if you are a first-time Doberman owner. It will not only teach your dog to yield his will to you, it will also teach you how to handle your dog with firmness and fairness. Dobermans are not tolerant of abusive training methods and can become mean and distrustful if they are treated with a heavy hand. Unlike some dogs who cower under mistreatment, the Doberman is more likely to become defensive. You might say the Doberman has a well-developed instinct for self-preservation. This dog demands kind and fair treatment, and he returns this respect tenfold. He wants to be your partner, not your adversary.

Loyalty

The personality trait that most endears the Doberman to his many admirers is his loyalty. He is not a subservient dog, and yet his whole purpose revolves around gaining the approval and acceptance of his master. He attaches his loyalty with such strong ties that he gives 200 percent to anything his master asks of him. His adoration for his owner easily becomes a mutual feeling between man and dog, which is why so many Doberman owners become hooked on the breed and subsequently go on to own others.

The personality trait that most endears the Doberman to his many admirers is his loyalty. His whole purpose revolves around gaining the approval and acceptance of his master.

Although he prefers to attach his strongest loyalties to the person who cares for him and trains him, the Doberman does not neglect other family members. He may make it his personal duty to watch over the children or anyone else he accepts into his protected circle. Other household members may have less influence on his behavior, but they are crucially important to him nonetheless.

An adult Doberman may take some time to transfer this loyalty to a new owner, as strong ties with an original owner do not dissolve easily. Obedience training classes are wonderfully effective in speeding up this process because the dog must first develop trust in his new owner before loyalty can blossom. Time and training can help integrate a Doberman of any age into his new home and family.

Friendliness

At the center of the Doberman's world is his owner, which necessarily puts others at a lesser status. Although some Dobermans may seem initially aloof toward strangers, this does not mean that they aren't friendly. In most cases, a Doberman simply needs to evaluate a person's intentions before accepting him as a friend.

When introduced properly and given a chance to size up a person, a Doberman will allow others into a personal relationship with him, sometimes treating friends as members of the family. But first impressions mean a lot. If someone intentionally or unintentionally intimidates or teases your Doberman, it may take a long time for him to learn to trust that person. The Doberman has a long memory for distrust, so proper introductions to new people are very important.

Unfortunately, most people are surprisingly ignorant of how to introduce themselves to an unfamiliar dog, so this responsibility will be in your hands. You will need to instruct new visitors how to conduct themselves so that your Doberman can accept them. Strangers should not display any intimidating body language, including lurching over your dog or raising a hand over your dog's head to pet him, unless your dog shows that he is comfortable with the person.

New acquaintances should allow your dog to sniff them, show your dog the back of their hand in a nonthreatening way, and wait for your dog to initiate friendly physical contact before petting. In most cases, it will only take a few seconds for your Doberman to determine a stranger's friendly intent, and then he will happily seek his new friend's attention.

Sensitivities

As a protective dog, the Doberman is very sensitive to loud noises or signs of aggression or violence. Fire feeds fire, so if a home is plagued with loud altercations or fits of human temper, he is likely to become very reactive to it. A Doberman needs a stable environment in which to nurture his sense of security and comfort, and he will not do well in an emotionally destructive home.

You might also find your Doberman sensitive to embarrassment or humiliation, if it's even possible to apply human emotions to dogs. This is a proud and dignified animal, and any harm to his pride will be evident in his sulky demeanor. A bath in tomato sauce after an encounter with a skunk is likely to hurt his pride immensely, as will laughing at his unintentional foibles. He definitely appreciates respect for his dignity!

Dominant Personality

Dogs with dominant personalities are produced within every breed, and the Doberman is no exception. Like people, some dogs are leaders and some are followers. This is nature's way of creating the hierarchy necessary for social animals to survive, and it is not necessarily a symptom of poor breeding. Dominant dogs of any breed, even pint-sized ones, can be a challenge to manage, but the dominant Doberman may be more so due to his size and strength. Any dog with this personality trait is not recommended for first-time owners, so care must be taken in choosing a pet with an appropriate temperament to match your knowledge, skill, and experience.

INTELLIGENCE

Don't let his working-dog looks fool you! The Doberman Pinscher is one of the most intelligent of dog breeds. This is a trait that has been bred into the Doberman since its early development because trainability was one of the characteristics most important to Louis Dobermann and his successors. While it is an admirable quality, the Doberman's active intellect demands plenty of attention and human interaction. Like most intelligent breeds, the Doberman can become bored and mischievous when he does not receive enough mental stimulation.

This makes the Doberman a wonderful choice for a companion if you enjoy the challenges and rewards of dog training. The Doberman is known to thrive on any number of obedience disciplines, including agility, flyball, canine freestyle, tracking, or schutzhund. He can master just about any task with the right amount of patience and practice. He loves to learn, has a heart for competition, and has the courage to meet obstacles with perseverance and determination. If you decide to pursue one of

Doberman IQ

The Doberman Pinscher is the fifth most intelligent breed of dog according to Stanley Coren's, *The Intelligence of Dogs*. Intelligence and trainability are characteristics that have been bred into the Doberman since Louis Dobermann began developing the breed in the 1870s.

these higher-level obedience sports, you will be amazed at your Doberman's capabilities.

He has proven his intellectual superiority by becoming useful in many different working capacities, including police work, drug detection, bomb detection, and arson detection. Many Dobermans have also become therapy dogs, guide dogs for the blind, movie stars, and circus act performers. You would be missing out on great possibilities if you did not explore the many training options available to test your dog's talents.

ACTIVITY LEVEL

Consistent with the Doberman's active intelligence is the vigor with which he approaches any challenge, whether intellectual or physical. The Doberman is a working dog, and as such, he has a desire to work and the stamina to perform a job. With a higher than average activity level, he does demand some time, attention, and adequate exercise. But if you enjoy an active lifestyle and would like to include a dog in your daily activities, a Doberman would surely love to join you.

The Doberman's appearance is a clue to his exercise requirements. Lean, well muscled, and possessing superior coordination, he relishes the opportunity to use his physical endowments. Not particularly suited to apartment life unless his physical needs can be met, he prefers enough space for a good

With an active intellect and a higher than average activity level, the Doberman demands lots of time, attention, and daily exercise.

romp now and then. Dobermans do enjoy pushing their physical abilities to the limit, and they will greet physical challenges with eagerness and spirit.

You should plan to spend at least 30 minutes twice a day providing a good aerobic workout for your dog. In lieu of providing an agility course, a good game of fetch or keep-away will help your dog expend his energy reserves in a positive way. Leash walking may be an enjoyable activity and great for socialization, but it is not the heart-pumping, adrenaline-packed

type of activity that Dobermans crave (and need) to keep their lithe bodies in shape. Jogging and cycling, however, are activities your Doberman will greet with enthusiasm.

LIVING ACCOMMODATIONS

Large and hardy, and having found popularity all over the world (including in countries with frigid climates), one might consider the Doberman Pinscher to be a good prospect for an outdoor dog. His short, smooth coat, however, lacks a protective undercoat to make him as weather-tolerant as other breeds. With little protection from the cold in winter and biting flies in summer, he is definitely not built for outdoor living.

On the other hand, his short, close-lying hair does make him an ideal prospect for an indoor dog. Even as a moderate shedder, this type of hair does not cling and can easily be brushed off clothing and furniture. It does not accumulate dirt and debris as easily as other canine coat types, which makes the Doberman an exceptionally clean household resident.

Besides his physical intolerance for the outdoors, the Doberman's loyal nature requires him to be in close proximity to those he loves. Living apart from his human pack could be socially depriving and therefore psychologically damaging. Dobermans in such a living situation can become untrusting, unpredictable, destructive, or aggressive. Genetics have preprogrammed him to be devoted and protective of his human charges, and being unable to fulfill this purpose can cause him much frustration and anxiety.

So, allow your Doberman to become a member of your family, share your home with him, and include him in your activities. You'll find him to be a vital, contributing member of your household.

COMPATIBILITY WITH CHILDREN

Doberman Pinschers are generally very good with children and make excellent family dogs, especially when raised in a family environment. Like any other dog, though, they may not have much tolerance for something they are not accustomed to, so they need to be socialized with children at a young age. When socialized properly, they are known for their gentleness and attachment to people.

Regardless of how well a dog responds to children, interactions should always be supervised. Children under the age of five do not always know how to play appropriately with animals, and constant guidance is necessary to prevent problems.

COMPATIBILITY WITH OTHER PETS

How well a dog gets along with other pets is often an individual rather than a breed trait that is influenced by both the dog's genetics and life experiences. Dobermans are usually very good with other household pets, provided that they receive positive experiences and are introduced properly. Introductions to other animals at a young age are very helpful in socializing a dog, and this can be accomplished by taking your dog for walks and participating in activities that include other animals. Young Dobermans, or those with an exceptionally high energy level, may have a greater tendency to harass other pets simply because they want attention and need something to do, but this does not involve intolerance or aggression. Providing adequate exercise can help lessen this tendency.

Now that you know what the Doberman Pinscher is about, both inside and out, you are well equipped to decide if this is the right breed for you. The Doberman offers a wealth of fine qualities for the person who appreciates what he is and can meet his needs for socialization, training, exercise, and care. For the right owner, he is the ultimate canine for companionship and protection and a dog worthy of pride, respect, and most importantly, love.

Dobermans are usually very good with other household pets provided that they have positive experiences with them and are properly introduced.

PREPARING

for Your Doberman Pinscher

D

o you feel tingles of anticipation? Have you spent days unable to think of anything else except the arrival of your new canine family member? What is it about getting a new dog or puppy that is so exciting? Maybe it's because puppies are so irresistible! Maybe you're anxious to get to know your new adult Doberman. Whether you are looking forward to the joys of having a puppy frolicking in the house, or settling in with an adult dog, the positive fulfillment of your expectations relies on choosing the right dog.

Mordecai Siegal's famous quote, "Acquiring a dog may be the only opportunity a human ever has to choose a relative," could not be more true. If chosen wisely, the right dog will fit into your home, family, and lifestyle as securely as a nut on a bolt. The wrong choice, however, may result in disharmony, stress, tension, conflict, and possibly separation. So it is important to put a lot of thought into choosing just the right dog for you and your family situation.

PUPPY OR ADULT?

There are advantages and disadvantages in getting either a puppy or an adult dog. You might prefer to start out with a puppy so you can enjoy the joys and rewards of puppyhood. Puppies are fun, playful, and irresistibly cute. Raising a puppy can give you the opportunity to socialize and train your dog from an early age, which will influence his behavior for the rest of his life. This is a valuable advantage if you want to socialize your dog with children or other pets in your household.

But these advantages do not come without a tradeoff. Puppies demand a lot of time, attention, and supervision. They are babies who have not yet learned their limits. They require a lot of training, including housetraining, crate training, and basic manners. And they need to be constantly supervised to prevent injuries and household damage. Puppies have a lot of energy and need plenty of opportunities to expend it in positive ways.

Beyond the cost of time and attention, puppies also demand a substantial financial commitment. In addition to the price of the puppy and his supplies, there are health

How to Choose Your Doberman

Many considerations go into choosing the right dog for you and your family. If you are trying to decide whether you want a puppy or an adult, take into account the following:

Choose a puppy if...

- you have the time and energy to devote to puppy rearing
- you want to socialize the puppy with children and pets already in the household
- you can make the financial commitment to care for the puppy properly

Choose an adult dog if...

- you would like a dog who already has some training, particularly housetraining
- you have a demanding lifestyle that is not conducive to puppy rearing
- you want a calmer, more mature dog

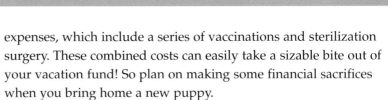

expenses, which include a series of vaccinations and sterilization surgery. These combined costs can easily take a sizable bite out of your vacation fund! So plan on making some financial sacrifices when you bring home a new puppy.

Adult dogs, on the other hand, are a good choice if you would rather bypass the demands of puppyhood. Dogs over a year old have outgrown the destructive teething stage and are often already housetrained. If they are adopted from a rescue or shelter, they have usually received the necessary vaccinations and have been neutered or spayed, which can significantly reduce first-year health expenses. A mature dog generally takes less time to train because he has a greater attention span than a puppy and is better able to retain what he learns. All of this adds up to a dog who will more easily fit into a family and household with a minimum of effort and expense.

The downside of getting an adult dog is that you will not have any control over the dog's upbringing. Inadequate socialization and improper handling can result in behavior issues that may need to be corrected. While some of these may be minor habits that can be resolved with training, more serious issues may require the guidance of a professional trainer or canine behaviorist.

It is important to evaluate the personality and behavior of any adult dog to be sure he is a good match for your family situation and to make sure any preexisting problems are manageable. Fortunately, dogs are very resilient and adaptable creatures.

Most problems encountered in getting an adult dog are no more challenging than the problems encountered in raising a puppy.

MALE OR FEMALE?

Experienced Doberman owners will admit slight personality or behavior differences between the sexes, most notably that males tend to be bolder (perhaps a good quality for dogs intended for sport use) and females tend to be more tolerant (a desirable trait for dogs intended as pets for families with children).

Your future goals should determine the sex of the dog you choose. If you simply want a good pet and plan to neuter or spay your dog, this decision is strictly a matter of personal preference because both sexes have the potential to become great companions. But if you are interested in participating in showing or breeding, there are a number of things you must consider before making a choice, one important consideration being the pros and cons of owning an unaltered dog.

Unaltered Females

Females go into heat twice per year, beginning at six to ten months of age. During the heat cycle, which lasts approximately one to two weeks, your dog will emit a bloody discharge and an odor (detectible by dogs) that can attract males from a mile or more away. The urge to mate is so compelling that you can expect occasional suitors to find their way to your doorstep, and there will always be the possibility of an accidental breeding.

You will need to carefully supervise your female when outdoors because even fences may not be enough to keep amorous dogs apart. But males are not the only ones affected by the female's estrous cycle. The female herself will also engage in sexual behaviors that are annoying or embarrassing. She may appear nervous or even slightly neurotic, or she may attempt to mount various objects, animals, or people.

Both males and females have the potential to become great companions.

Unaltered Males

An unaltered male will present his own challenges. He will not go into heat, but his sexual behavior is often more difficult to manage. Unlike a female, who becomes sexually active twice per year, a male is always on sexual alert, waiting to act on any opportunity that presents itself. This results in a high incidence of roaming, marking territory by eliminating on vertical objects (sometimes in the house), and mounting just about anything when the urge hits him, including the legs of your guests.

These kinds of behaviors can be embarrassing at the least and dangerous at the most. Because stud fees are usually insufficient to pay for damage to your home or fines when your dog is caught roaming, managing an unaltered male is also best left to those who take showing and breeding seriously and are willing to invest in the necessary precautions.

Quality Is the Best Deal

Professional breeders are obviously the best source for quality Doberman puppies, but if you think the cost is beyond your means, here is a good rule of thumb: Purchase the best dog you can possibly afford, even if your intentions are simply to have a good pet. Health expenses related to poor breeding can quickly turn your bargain dog into a money pit! More importantly, the money you save will not be enough to compensate for the cost of your heartache.

WHERE TO FIND THE DOG OF YOUR DREAMS

The Doberman Pinscher has maintained a good standing in breed popularity for many years, so you do not need the skills of Sherlock Holmes to find one. There are a number of reliable sources for dogs that you can investigate, depending on the quality of dog you seek, how much you want to spend, and whether you want a puppy or an adult.

Professional Breeders

Professional breeders are individuals who are serious about producing the best quality dogs according to the breed standard. They are often involved in conformation competition, and their breeding stock may have won conformation titles. This type of breeder can be located through local Doberman Pinscher clubs, veterinarians, or by attending local dog shows.

Professional breeders evaluate the looks, temperament, and health of their breeding stock so that the progeny of their dogs are superior representatives of the breed. Such breeding practices include keeping a close tab on any genetic defects and culling any dogs from the breeding program who do not meet high standards for health and temperament.

Choose a breeder whose puppies appear healthy and happy and whose facilities are well maintained.

Advantages of Professional Breeders

Because special care is taken in breeding only the best dogs, a professional breeder will usually provide health and temperament guarantees, a valuable benefit not always offered through other sources. If you are looking for a show-quality dog, this should be the only source you consider. The track record of the parent dogs is an important indicator of how suitable a puppy will be for showing. Puppies bred for the correct conformation are also good prospects for other activities because they will be well balanced and physically sound.

Purchasing a puppy from a professional breeder will give you the opportunity to evaluate the parent dogs. Even if the breeder acquired stud service elsewhere, the dam will be available to give you an indication of at least half of the inheritable genes acquired by the puppies. Keep in mind that pregnancy and birth necessarily take a toll on a dog's body, and it's not unusual for a lactating female to appear in poor condition with weight or hair loss. The purpose of inspecting her is not to judge her postpartum condition but to evaluate her structure and temperament.

Professional breeders also use sale contracts. This offers advantages for both you and the breeder. It outlines the responsibilities of both parties so that misunderstandings can

Reviewing a Breeder's Sale Contract

Breeders often draft their own contracts, so requirements and guarantees can vary considerably from one source to another. It is important to review any sale contract thoroughly prior to signing it. Make sure that you understand all the provisions and requirements in the contract and ask questions if anything is unclear.

- Are the health guarantees broad enough to cover genetic defects and health conditions that may show up in the future?
- What kind of return, exchange, or refund policies are offered?
- Are the requirements for the buyer reasonable or unrealistic?
- What are the penalties for breach of contract?
- Which state laws apply to the interpretation of the contract?

be avoided. Unfortunately, no standard sale contract exists, and breeders often draft their own, which means the requirements and guarantees can vary considerably from one contract to another. It is important to review any sale contract thoroughly prior to signing it.

Disadvantages of Professional Breeders

Perhaps the greatest disadvantage of getting a Doberman puppy from a professional breeder is the cost. Puppies from this source command top dollar, but like any other commodity, you get what you pay for. There are always a few pet-quality puppies produced by professional breeders; these animals may have slight imperfections in color or conformation that make them unsuitable for a show career. Although offered at reduced prices, the cost may still be higher than pet-quality Dobermans available through other sources.

Evaluating a Professional Breeder

Price alone does not determine the quality of a dog. It is important to evaluate a breeder and keep a close eye on detail because this will help you judge the quality of the breeder, which in turn reflects the quality and value of the puppies.

Serious breeders always breed registered dogs and keep pedigree and health records to track the success of their breeding efforts. These records should be available to you upon request. A quality breeder will also provide a clean, healthy environment in which her puppies thrive, and she will spend time handling and socializing the puppies from the moment they are born.

If a breeder offers puppies younger than eight weeks old for sale, you can bet she is not a professional. Puppies should not be sold until they are at least eight to ten weeks old because they acquire important social skills from their mother and littermates during this time. Puppies of any age should be current with vaccinations and dewormings. If a breeder neglects to engage in any one of these practices, you would be wise to take your business elsewhere.

Commercial Breeders

Commercial breeders produce purebred puppies for the purpose of making a profit. They may operate smaller, privately owned breeding kennels, or large commercial breeding facilities that sell directly to the public or to pet shops. Usually found through newspaper ads, the phone book, or other forms of advertising, they can be a good source of affordable purebred dogs, but you won't find any outstanding representations of the breed here.

Advantages of Commercial Breeders

Commercial breeders can afford to offer purebred puppies at significantly lower prices. They do not have strict requirements for buyers, and they usually have plenty of puppies from which

Reputable breeders will socialize their puppies from a young age.

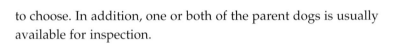

Evaluating a Breeder

Before you acquire your dog, be sure to do your homework. A good breeder will let you visit and spend some time at her facility. She will also welcome any questions you may have. Here are some important things to consider:

- Are the puppies registered with a reputable registry?
- Are pedigree records available?
- Is a sale contract available, and does it provide adequate health or temperament guarantees?
- Are the puppies at least eight to ten weeks old?
- Have the puppies received their first set of vaccinations and a deworming treatment?
- Are the puppies kept in a clean environment?
- Are the puppies handled and socialized frequently with people?
- Are one or both of the parent dogs available for inspection?

It is beneficial for both you and your breeder to learn more about each other before you make decisions or sign an agreement on a dog of your choice.

to choose. In addition, one or both of the parent dogs is usually available for inspection.

Disadvantages of Commercial Breeders

Even though puppies from this source are usually registered, they are unlikely to be show quality. This is strictly a source for pet-quality dogs. Smaller commercial breeders are more likely to afford proper socialization and care for their puppies than large-scale operations.

A handful of large-scale breeding facilities are quite respectable. They are discriminatory in their breeding practices, provide meticulously clean living conditions, and offer outstanding health and temperament guarantees. But unfortunately, the great majority of large-scale breeding operations are considered "puppy mills."

The breeding dogs in puppy mills may be kept in substandard conditions, and the puppies may not receive adequate socialization. The breeding practices of puppy mills also leave much to be desired, with many of the puppies inheriting genetic defects or health conditions. Avoid purchasing a puppy from a puppy mill at all costs because the affordable price of the puppy will not be enough to compensate for the cost of your heartache. The physical and psychological problems associated with puppies from this source are most often irreversible.

Evaluating a Commercial Breeder

Just because commercial breeders are in the business of making money does not necessarily mean they are disreputable, but the same criteria used to evaluate a professional breeder applies. The puppies should be in good health and live in a clean environment. Pedigree records should be available to determine if inbreeding is present. At least one parent dog should be available for inspection, and the puppies should be no less than eight weeks old and have the appropriate vaccinations and dewormings. If a puppy sale contract is not available, request health or temperament guarantees in writing.

Hobby Breeders

Also known as backyard breeders, hobby breeders are dog owners who choose to breed their own pets. The majority of newspaper classified ads feature puppies from this source.

Advantages of Hobby Breeders

The quality of the puppies produced by hobby breeders depends on the knowledge of the breeder. Those who have done their research to produce genetically sound dogs with the correct physical and temperament traits are capable of producing dogs with show potential. If their breeding stock comes from championship lines and they hire the services of a respected stud dog with traits that will benefit his progeny, the quality of the puppies will be superior. It is possible to obtain a very good quality dog at a reasonable price from a conscientious hobby breeder.

Disadvantages of Hobby Breeders

Unfortunately, most hobby breeders are *not* meticulous in planning their breeding strategies. More than likely, they are dog owners who decide to breed their pet with a neighbor's dog who just happens to be of the same breed. They might allow their own male and female dogs to breed, regardless of the suitability of the parents to produce good-quality puppies, or they will choose stud services according to cost or convenience. Most puppies obtained from hobby breeders are not destined to be star material.

A shelter or breed rescue can be a great source if you are looking to acquire an adult Doberman.

Evaluating a Hobby Breeder

To determine their respectability, hobby breeders should be evaluated with the same scrutiny that applies to any other breeder. Even though the puppies may not be registered or have pedigree information available, the age of the pups, appropriate veterinary care, living conditions, socialization, and parent dog inspection are vitally important.

Because temperament is such an important quality in the Doberman, scrutinize the parent dogs carefully prior to purchasing a puppy, even if the puppy is only intended as a pet. Hobby breeders do not always provide a purchase contract, so health and temperament guarantees should be requested in writing. If a breeder is unwilling to provide any guarantees, you are wise to turn your tail in another direction. Even when the price seems right, a poorly bred Doberman can become a source of great expense and heartache if he suffers from temperament problems or inheritable health conditions.

Animal Shelters

Most people associate unwanted dogs with undesirable dogs, but you would be surprised how many treasures can be found in an animal shelter! Do not automatically exclude a shelter dog from consideration because many dogs find themselves in shelters due to no fault of their own.

In some cases, the dog's owner has died. In other cases, people who do not take the time to train their pets find themselves frustrated and subsequently relinquish their pets to shelters. Many dogs, especially those who are not neutered or spayed, are picked up as strays and are never reunited with their owners. In other words, most shelter dogs are good dogs who simply lack a good home.

Advantages of Animal Shelters

A shelter can be a great source if you are looking to acquire an adult Doberman because the majority of relinquished dogs are in the one- to two-year age group, a perfect age to assimilate into your household and begin obedience training. Adoption fees are much more affordable than purchasing a purebred dog from any other source, and most shelters take care of vaccinations and neutering prior to releasing a dog to a new home.

Disadvantages of Animal Shelters

Even though the Humane Society of the United States estimates that 25 percent of the dogs in shelters are purebreds, it may be a challenge to locate a Doberman, much less the *right* Doberman for your needs. Most shelter dogs come without registration papers, pedigrees, or health records, and those who are acquired as strays have completely unknown histories. Without this information, there are no guarantees against hereditary defects or temperament problems.

A chance also exists that a shelter dog developed some behavior issues that led to his relinquishment. Unfortunately, poorly bred dogs with aggression-related problems often find their way into shelters, and these animals should be strictly avoided. The good news is that most problem behaviors can be corrected with proper training. However, it is important to be aware of any problems prior to adopting and to seek the necessary support and advice to correct them.

Breed Rescues

Breed rescues are nonprofit organizations that provide shelter and adoption services for dogs of a particular breed. They usually operate as a network of foster homes, but otherwise function much the same as an animal shelter. Breed registries and Doberman Pinscher Clubs can refer you to a Doberman rescue organization in your area.

Advantages of Breed Rescues

Because Doberman rescues specialize in the breed, it is obviously easier to find the right Doberman for you. Rescue staff and volunteers have a lot of knowledge and experience with the breed, which translates into a source of expert advice, information, and superior evaluations of dogs and adopters. The dogs sheltered by rescues tend to receive more individualized care and attention than those in animal shelters because they are kept in foster homes. Living in a home environment, as opposed to being kept in a kennel, sheds more light on a dog's behavior, personality, and household manners.

Overall, Doberman rescues are the most desirable source to locate an adoptable, adult who will be the best match for your family. Even though adoption fees tend to be slightly higher than those of animal shelters, the cost is still very reasonable when you consider that vaccinations and sterilization surgery are usually included.

Disadvantages of Breed Rescues

Like shelter dogs, rescued Dobermans are unlikely to have registration papers, health records, or detailed histories. They may have behavior or temperament issues that must be considered, and there are no guarantees against hereditary health or temperament problems. Even so, the rewards of adopting a homeless dog are priceless, and you may very well find that an adopted Doberman develops an especially close relationship with his owner.

Internet Sources

Technology has provided new options in the purchase of purebred dogs, that being

The Adoption Process

During the adoption process, shelter volunteers will interview applicants to make sure that they can handle all the responsibilities involved in dog ownership. Their job is to ensure the best possible matches for both the dogs and their new owners. Some of the routine questions asked include:

- How many people live in your household?
- What are their ages?
- Is everyone in favor of adopting a dog at this time?
- How much time will your dog spend outdoors?
- On a scale of 1 to 10, how much dog training experience do you have?
- How important is it to you that your dog gets along well with other dogs?
- Do you plan to participate in any organized activities with him?

These owner surveys are designed to give the counselor a clear picture of the kind of dog you want and the type of owner you will be.

You will have also have an opportunity to ask any questions you may have about the dogs you are considering. Here are some things to ask that may help you to make your final decision:

- What is the age (or estimated age) of the dog?
- Does the dog have any medical problems?
- What is the dog's temperament like?
- What is known about the dog's history?
- How many homes has this dog had?
- Is the dog housetrained?
- Is there evidence of any previous obedience training?
- Is there evidence of any previous abuse or neglect?
- Why was the dog surrendered?

You should always ask these and any other questions you may have in order to make the most informed adoption decision possible.

Once you complete an application, it may be as long as week before you are approved and able to take a dog home. Expect to spend at least a few hours speaking with the shelter staff and meeting different dogs. If the dog you select has not been spayed or neutered yet, this also must be done before homecoming day. You may not even find the dog you're looking for right away. In this case, the shelter can contact you when more dogs become available. Most facilities admit new animals on a regular basis.

Source: The Happy Adopted Dog, *TFH Publications, Inc.*

the ability to locate and purchase puppies or dogs online. Breeders and hobby breeders in particular may offer the opportunity to purchase dogs via the Internet and deliver them or ship them directly to you. This method of selling and delivering dogs has its own advantages and disadvantages.

It has never been easier to locate the exact type of dog you desire. Regardless of your preferences, you can find precisely what you want anywhere in the country—or the world! Doing business online can be easy and efficient, and it provides more options than may be available locally. Nevertheless, some disadvantages must be considered. Buying a puppy isn't quite as simple as filling out an online order form. Evaluating the puppy or his parents in person is usually not practical or possible. Shipping a dog or puppy long distances can be stressful or traumatic for the animal, especially if he encounters delivery delays. In addition, if any sale contract disputes arise, they usually have to be settled in a court of law located within the breeder's state of residence. This can cause significant problems for the buyer, who may reside in a state across the country.

Internet use has some practical applications, however. Locating breeders, animal shelters, and breed rescues statewide and within surrounding states can expand the available pool of dogs from which to choose. Contacting and communicating with these sources online is easy and inexpensive. For those who are willing to travel in this wider area to inspect a prospect personally, there is a greater chance they will be able to locate just the right dog.

EVALUATING A PUPPY

Regardless of where you decide to get your puppy, evaluate him for health and temperament before plunking down your hard-earned cash to finalize a sale. This puppy will be an investment into a long-term relationship that can bring either boundless joy or excruciating heartache into your life. Imagine your disappointment to discover your precious pup has serious health or temperament issues!

A Doberman puppy who is friendly but slightly reserved will often have a stable and intelligent temperament.

Health

Evaluate each puppy as an individual, and check closely for any signs of illness prior to purchase. Lethargy, diarrhea, and a bloated belly may be signs of parasite infestation. Weepy eyes, discharge from the nose, or poor skin and coat condition are most certainly symptoms of a virus or a potentially serious illness. If any puppies in a litter are ill, chances are that they have all contracted the same illness even if they don't all show symptoms. In these cases, walk away. It may be extremely difficult to leave behind a pup who captured your heart at first sight, but your future happiness depends on listening to your head, not your heart.

Temperament

A litter of puppies is as entertaining as a comedy troupe. All puppies are funny, charming, and playful—they all have wonderful personalities, right? Although all puppies engage in typical puppy behaviors, they do not all have the same personality. You need to remember that puppies spend a very short part of their lives as babies, and your puppy will eventually grow up to become an adult with whom you will spend many years. So it is vitally important to predict, as accurately as possible, whether a puppy will become the kind of adult you can live with happily.

When evaluating puppies for temperament, some people subscribe to the mistaken notion that the boldest, most outgoing puppy in a litter will make the best pet. Others tend to fall for the small, shy runt of the litter whose diminutive appeal is difficult to resist. Experts, however, suggest avoiding temperament extremes and choosing a puppy who falls somewhere in between. Look for a puppy who is friendly, but slightly reserved, and who shows a desire to analyze a situation prior to acting. This little guy will have a stable and intelligent temperament.

Enough emphasis cannot be made on choosing a Doberman with a suitable temperament. A Doberman puppy who is extremely dominant will prove to be exceptionally challenging to train, even in the hands of a very experienced dog owner. Extremely shy Dobermans may have difficulty developing trust, especially toward strangers, and can develop the very dangerous habit of fear biting. Temperament extremes in the Doberman have a greater potential to cause problems than those in other breeds of dog.

EVALUATING AN ADULT DOG

It is much easier to evaluate the health and temperament of adult dogs. No longer a litter member, an adult dog will not harbor invisible symptoms of illness originating from his littermates. If an adult is sick, symptoms will most likely be apparent.

Health

When purchasing or adopting an adult dog, check him over from head to tail to detect any problems. The eyes should be clear and alert. The ears should be clean without signs of discharge, redness, swelling, or sensitivity. Check the mouth and teeth for inflammation of the gums and tartar buildup. Lift each paw to check the pads of the feet for injuries. Check under the tail and run your hands over the entire body to feel for lumps or skin tumors.

A thorough body check not only helps detect any physical problems, it will also tell you how well the adult dog accepts the handling of his various body parts. Resisting and pulling away from you is normal for a dog who is not used to being handled, but an aggressive reaction may indicate a temperament problem.

Temperament

It helps to bring treats and toys with you when evaluating an adult dog. You can reward the dog for good behavior during the physical check, and you can also use food and toys to determine

Registering Your Dog

If your dog is eligible for registration with the American Kennel Club (AKC) or the Kennel Club (KC), you want to submit the appropriate paperwork as soon as possible so these organizations have updated ownership information.

To register your Doberman puppy with the AKC, obtain an AKC Dog Registration Application from the seller. This should be available at the time of sale. Because the AKC requires a litter of puppies to be registered by the breeder before any of the individual puppies can be registered, lack of appropriate paperwork at the time of sale may indicate that the puppies are not eligible for registration. What does this mean for you? It means you should never accept promises that registration application papers will be forthcoming when you purchase a dog because they are unlikely to arrive!

Once obtained and completed, send the application to the AKC with the appropriate registration fee to obtain your dog's AKC Registration Certificate. If your dog already has an AKC Registration Certificate, you can complete the new owner information on the certificate and submit it with the correct fee to obtain a new certificate.

Registering your Doberman with the KC isn't quite as complicated because the breeder is responsible for registering the individual puppies. The buyer simply needs to complete the transfer of ownership information on the registration certificate and submit it to the KC with the appropriate fee to obtain an updated certificate.

how well he is trained and how much he is motivated by these kinds of rewards. Lack of training is, by no means, a reason to discount a dog as an adoption prospect because you can provide any necessary training yourself. It is the dog's interest in learning and his willingness to be trained that are important.

A dog who shows no interest in people, ignores you, or abandons the lure of a tasty treat will be difficult, if not impossible, to train. If he shows possessiveness of the food or toys, he may have a problem with dominance aggression or food aggression. Just as with puppies, adult Dobermans with temperament extremes should be avoided.

PREPARING FOR YOUR DOG

Puppies are curious and fearless little creatures who have a lot of energy and tend to get into plenty of mischief. They like to explore, taste, chew, and play with anything within their reach. While their behavior is quite endearing, it also poses the risk of accidents, injuries, and damage to your property. Preparing your home for your puppy's arrival can help reduce this risk and make living with him a little less stressful.

Pet-proof your home and yard to ensure your puppy's safety. Areas designated for eating, sleeping, and play should be free of potential hazards, such as toxic plants.

Pet-Proofing Your Home

Puppy-proofing your home consists of detecting and removing any hazards, such as exposed electrical cords, houseplants, and toxic materials. If you get down on your hands and knees to survey your home from your puppy's point of view, you'd be surprised how many potential hazards you can find! Garbage should be covered or moved to an inaccessible spot. Toys, shoes, clothing, or other items should be safely stored in closets to prevent damage. Getting a puppy is the best reason you've ever had to keep your home clean and free of clutter.

An adult dog, although usually past the chewing stage of development and not as apt to get into as much trouble as a puppy, may still chew on select items that strike his fancy. Your home is just as new to him, and it will take at least two weeks for him to adjust to his new living arrangements and feeding schedule. He still has to be taught which items and areas are taboo, and this process can be streamlined by removing any tempting objects from reach.

Designating Responsibilities

Preparing for a new puppy or dog involves some advance planning. Who will have the responsibility of feeding your dog? Where will his food and water dishes be kept? Where will his food be stored? Where will he sleep? Where will he be kept when no one is at home? Where will he be taken to relieve himself, and who will be responsible for cleaning up after him?

If possible, make dog care chores a family effort. Helping to care for a canine family member is a wonderful learning opportunity for children. If you keep the chores fun and rewarding, you can prevent protests and complaints. Emphasize the dog's joy at feeding time, turn yard cleanup into a search game, and show how grooming can produce a beautiful dog of whom you can all be proud.

Threatening to get rid of your dog when the children become lax in their duties will not encourage participation. There is always the possibility that, no matter how fun you have tried to make caring for the dog, your children will lose interest, and it will become a battle of wills to get chores done. Keep in mind that prodding may be necessary, and the possibility always exists that you will have to assume all the dog care responsibilities yourself. Keeping a dog should not be reliant on the help of your children.

Designating Areas

Organization prevents chaos, and who needs chaos in an already stressful world? Everything should have a place, and designating specific areas for your dog to eat, sleep, and potty, as well as designating restricted areas, can make your life more efficient and reduce your dog-care load. No one wants to clean dog food off the carpet or have to search the entire yard to keep it clean of excrement.

Where to Feed Your Dog

Deciding where to feed your new dog or puppy is a matter of convenience. Choose a spot that has flooring that is easy to keep clean. Kitchens or laundry rooms are good choices, but food and water dishes should be located away from major traffic patterns. Dobermans are notorious for splattering and dribbling their drinking water, and it's no fun to step in or slip on puddles.

If you have other dogs, figure out how to feed them separately because feeding them near each other may create competition for food. This can result in one dog getting the lion's share and the other left with barely enough to maintain his weight. You can manage this problem by feeding your dogs in their crates or in separate rooms. This also makes it much easier to keep track of how much each dog is eating.

Sleeping Arrangements

Puppies may need to be kept in a crate or puppy pen at night to prevent nighttime accidents, but they still prefer to be near their people. Your bedroom may seem like the ideal place, but your nighttime peace may be shattered by the cries of a lonely puppy who misses his mother and littermates. These nocturnal interruptions will usually subside as your puppy adjusts to his new home, and plenty of exercise prior to bedtime can help encourage your puppy to sleep at night. But if you find it difficult to function after several nights of sporadic sleep, it might be best to bed your puppy down in another room.

Adult dogs need a soft, warm bed to curl up on, and this should be placed in an area free from drafts and dampness. Avoid putting your dog's bed under a window or in a room that is not properly heated or ventilated. A good-quality bed will contribute to your dog's good health and prevent the development of unsightly, hairless calluses, of which shorthaired dogs like the Doberman are prone. Dobermans who spend too much time lying on hard surfaces will wear the hair off their elbows, hips, and other areas where bones protrude. The skin in these areas will eventually thicken to cause permanent damage to the hair follicles and permanent hair loss.

Off-Limits Areas

Other designated areas may include places that are off limits to your puppy. You may not want him to play on your expensive Persian carpet or get into the garbage in the utility room. You may need to gate him out of areas where other animals are fed or where litter boxes are kept. Determining in advance which areas will be off limits will make it easier to manage and train your puppy consistently from the moment he arrives.

Potty Area

Perhaps the most important designated area is the potty area. Choosing a specific outdoor location where your puppy will be taken to relieve himself not only makes cleanup a little easier, it also helps tremendously with housetraining. Your puppy will soon learn the purpose of this particular area, and the scents there will encourage him to continue using it for that purpose.

Supplies and Equipment

Getting a new dog or puppy is an exciting and sometimes spontaneous event. When contact with a shelter or breeder reveals the availability of a Doberman for sale or adoption, your heart starts racing and you leap into action, for there's no telling how quickly the dog will be adopted or how many puppies will be left

Help Your Puppy Sleep

If your puppy whiles away the night wailing, he may need your assistance to settle into a blissful slumber. Make sure he receives plenty of exercise prior to bedtime so he'll be tired enough to sleep. A warm water bottle wrapped in a towel or a stuffed toy can become welcome surrogates for nighttime cuddling. The steady rhythm of a clock or a metronome can also help lull your little fellow into dreamland.

by the time you get there. This is one of the drawbacks of choosing such a popular breed!

Even so, you probably entertained the idea of getting a new dog well in advance. Perhaps you've wanted a Doberman Pinscher for quite some time. If you have committed to this decision, make a list of all the items you will need to care for a dog prior to actually getting one. Any items that can be purchased in advance will minimize your running around at the last minute to acquire everything you need.

Collar

A Doberman puppy will need an adjustable collar that can be enlarged as he grows. It should be checked frequently to make sure it has not become too tight. A well-fitted collar should rotate easily around your puppy's neck, but should not be so loose that he can slip out of it or get it caught in his mouth. An adult Doberman needs a collar that fits correctly as well. You should be able to fit two fingers between the collar and your dog's neck. Leather or nylon buckle collars are good choices that can be kept on your dog at all times. A helpful tip: Rolled collars are narrower and will cause less chafing and hair loss for your thin-coated Doberman.

A collar needs to be properly fitted for safety and comfort. An adjustable nylon collar is a good choice for a Doberman puppy.

Leash

For dog walking or training, a 6-foot (1.8-m) leash is a necessity. Keep your dog's size in mind when choosing a leash. Although you can get by with a 0.5-inch (1.5-cm) wide leash for a puppy, your adult Doberman should have a leather or nylon leash at least 0.75- (1.9-cm) to 1-inch (2.5-cm) wide.

Food and Water Bowls

An adult Doberman will need food and water bowls that hold approximately two quarts (1.9 liters). Puppies can use smaller bowls to start. A tremendous variety of pet bowls are on the market, from fancy to practical, but the most important qualities to keep in mind are: Is it dishwasher safe,

and is it slip-proof and tip-proof? Ease of care is the name of the game in this busy world.

Food and Water

If you can purchase the brand of food your dog received before you got him, you can make his transition to his new home easier and less stressful. Make sure you have some bottled water on hand, too, because some dogs refuse to drink water that smells or tastes different from what they're accustomed to.

Crate

A crate is most certainly recommended for puppies, both for security and training. It should be large enough for your puppy to stand, turn around, and lie down in comfortably. To avoid having to purchase different size crates as your puppy grows, you can purchase a large crate and section off the excess space.

An adult Doberman may or may not need a crate, depending on the dog and your home situation. A crate large enough to hold an adult dog obviously takes up a lot of room, but may be necessary if you need to feed pets separately or keep your dog confined for short periods of time. In this case, it may be desirable to purchase a collapsible crate that can be moved out of the way when it is not in use. The same rules apply where size is concerned: The crate should be large enough for your adult dog to stand, turn around, and lie down in comfortably.

Doggy Bed

Large dogs do not always make good bed partners or couch companions due to the space they take up, so it is important to provide your dog with a comfortable place of his own to retire. As discussed, Dobermans, being prone to ugly calluses when forced to lie on hard surfaces, should have an exceptionally thick, good-quality dog bed.

Be wary of cedar-filled beds, which are not washable and cause allergic reactions in some dogs. Dobermans are particularly clean dogs, without the doggy odor attributed to some breeds, so odor-control quality is not a priority in making your choice. It is more important to select a bed that can be easily washed.

Shopping List

Before bringing your puppy or dog to his new home, you must prepare for his arrival. The following are some basic supplies you will need:

- boundary spray
- brushes and combs
- chew toys
- collar
- dog treats
- doggy bed
- food
- food and water bowls
- identification tag
- leash
- nail clippers
- pet carrier
- pooper-scooper
- stain/odor remover

All dogs need toys. Aside from providing activity and exercise, they can be extremely useful in training your new pet and steering him away from problem behaviors.

Grooming Tools

Assemble a starter grooming kit that includes a rubber curry brush, a soft-bristled brush, medium or large nail clippers, and a chamois skin (if desired). Other grooming supplies, such as shampoo and bathing equipment, ear cleaning products, and oral care products, can be purchased during subsequent shopping trips.

Deterrent Spray

Deterrent sprays can help enforce household rules and make your dog's adjustment to his new home proceed more smoothly— not to mention making *your* life much easier! Sprays intended for both indoor and outdoor use can help mark areas or furniture that are off limits and prevent chewing damage. Be sure to follow the product directions carefully.

Pooper-Scooper

It's not a pleasant job, but someone has to do it! You might as well make cleaning up after your dog as easy and efficient as possible. A long-handled pooper-scooper is a real back-saver and well worth the investment.

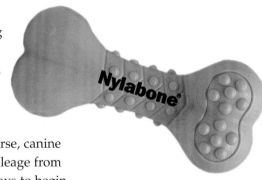

Toys and Treats

A dog can never have too many toys, but of course, canine playthings can be quite expensive. Get the most mileage from your investment by purchasing different types of toys to begin with: a rope for tuggers, a ball for fetchers, and toys with different chewing textures for chewers, such as the ones made by Nylabone. You will quickly learn what kind of toys your dog prefers. If your

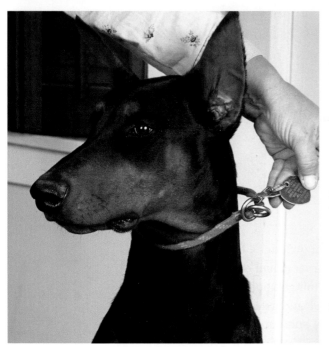

Identification tags will help your dog find his way home should he become lost.

Doberman is a heavy chewer, avoid soft rubber or fabric toys that can be easily shredded or consumed.

Experiment with different types of treats to find one that motivates your dog without getting him overly excited. Consumable bones, such as rawhide, can be provided in small quantities, but some dogs do not digest these easily. Beef shank bones are a welcome treat for adult Dobermans, but purchase the longer ones—more than one dog has been known to get his jaw stuck through the hole of the shorter bones. And never give your dog pork bones or other softer types of bones that can splinter and cause internal problems.

Identification

One of the most important pet care items you will need to obtain does not involve food, shelter, or grooming. Losing a pet or having a beloved pet stolen are among the most heartbreaking experiences a dog owner can suffer. Unfortunately, pet loss or theft occurs much more often than we want to imagine. It doesn't take long to become extremely attached to your new canine family member—or to lose him.

The following forms of identification will help your dog find his way home in the event he is lost or stolen. Do your research ahead of time and decide which method you prefer because you will need to take care of this soon after bringing your dog home.

ID Tags: The first line of defense against preventing your dog from becoming irretrievably lost is to put ID tags on his collar. This is the most easily recognizable form of identification for someone who might find your missing dog. In addition to a personalized tag with your name and phone number on it, be sure to obtain your dog's license tag as soon as possible. A dog license not only provides a good form of identification, it is required by ordinance in most communities.

Microchipping: As valuable as pet tags are for identification purposes, they are not infallible. Collars can fall off, or thieves can easily remove them. Most experts recommend using at least one other form of identification in addition to ID tags, the most popular and technologically advanced of which is microchipping.

Microchipping is a method of identification that involves injecting a small, rice-sized capsule containing a computer chip under the skin between the shoulder blades. This is a quick and relatively painless procedure that can be performed by your veterinarian. Many agencies responsible for the collection of stray and lost pets will, as a matter of practice, use a scanner to detect microchips in the animals who find their way to these facilities. An added benefit is that most educational institutions and laboratory facilities will not purchase microchipped dogs for experimentation purposes.

The major drawback of microchipping is that it is not a visible form of identification and cannot be detected without a scanner. Because most people do not own scanners, this form of identification is effective only when your dog comes into the hands of the right people. Another problem is that microchips are produced by a number of manufacturers, and scanners are not capable of reading all the different microchips on the market. Manufacturers are currently conducting discussions on how these products can be standardized, but meanwhile it has left an older form of permanent identification as a viable alternative: tattooing.

Tattooing: Tattooing is a relatively painless procedure involving the injection of ink under the skin. Letters, numbers, or a combination of both can be tattooed under the ear, on the belly, or inside a rear leg to provide a visible, life-long form of identification. But there are drawbacks to this, too, because tattoos can become blurred and illegible with age, hair can grow over them, or those who wish to erase your dog's identity can alter them. Even so, tattooing remains the only visible form of permanent identification available.

PET SITTING OPTIONS

Dogs are considered a high-maintenance pet, which means they require much more intensive care than other types of pets. Getting a dog involves making a commitment to meet the responsibilities of dog ownership, which includes providing food, water, shelter,

Questions to Ask a Prospective Pet Sitter

Finding the correct pet sitter is no different than finding a competent person to take care of a child. Remember, just because people call themselves pet sitters doesn't necessarily mean that they are qualified for the job. It's your responsibility to check each candidate's credentials. Here are some good questions to ask:

- How many years of experience do you have?
- How much experience do you have with Doberman Pinschers?
- Are you a member of a professional organization?
- What are your emergency procedures?
- Do you provide a written contract for services?
- Are you insured and bonded?
- Can you provide any references?
- Who will back you up in the event of an emergency on your end?

and exercise. These duties cannot be neglected without affecting the physical and emotional well-being of your dog.

It can be a challenge to meet all these needs consistently, especially if you have a demanding career and family obligations. You might also find yourself in an emergency situation that requires your absence. Who will care for your dog when you can't?

A number of pet sitting options are available to fill in the gaps. Each one has its own advantages and disadvantages, and your individual situation will determine which option is best for you and your dog. Websites for professional pet sitting organizations, such as the National Association of Professional Pet Sitters (NAPPS) at www.napps.org, or Pet Sitters International (PSI) at www.psi.org, maintain membership databases that can help you locate a pet sitter in your area. It's always best to have this information available to you *before* an unexpected need arises.

In-Home Pet Sitters

In-home pet sitters have become a very popular source of pet care in a variety of situations. In addition to providing backup care when you go on vacation, in-home pet sitters also offer midday walks that can help your dog expend some energy and get an extra potty break while you are at work or away from home for the day. This can be a real plus if your dog has urinary problems or if you tend to work long hours. In-home pet sitters can also help with health care needs, such as dispensing medications or checking on your dog when he is recuperating from an injury or surgery.

When you're on vacation, in-home pet sitters can provide services not available through boarding kennels or other pet sitting arrangements. They can water plants, bring in the mail, and perform other household duties while you are gone. Best of all, your dog is allowed to remain in the familiar, comfortable surroundings of his own home.

The only problem with this type of service is that Dobermans are known to take their duty as property guardians very seriously. A pet sitter can't do her job if your dog won't let her into the house! The pet sitter—preferably a woman, as your Doberman may be more wary if a strange man attempts to enter your house—may have to make a number of visits while you are present so your dog can learn to feel comfortable letting her enter and exit the premises. Once trained to accept a particular pet sitter's care, any dog can benefit from this type of service.

As with any pet care service, in-home pet sitters should be evaluated for qualifications and experience. There is no regulatory control over this type of business, so it is up to you to exercise good judgment in choosing a care provider. Although it is not necessarily an indication of quality, the pet sitter's membership in a professional organization such as NAPPS or PSI does show the provider takes her job seriously and is committed to professionalism.

Services should be outlined in a written contract, and the pet sitter should be insured and bonded. When evaluating a pet sitting service, the pet sitter should make a home visit to become acquainted with your dog and to acquire pertinent information about his health, habits, and special needs.

Boarding Kennels

Traditional boarding kennels used to be one of the few options available to those who required extended care for their dogs. Historically, living facilities at boarding kennels were restricted to indoor kennels and outdoor runs with a minimum of creature comforts—conditions that, by today's standards, would be likened to canine incarceration. Many modern boarding kennels, however, have embraced the trends of specialized care, comfortable accommodations, and opportunities for exercise, stimulation, and socialization.

If you are away from home often or can't take your dog with you when you travel, a qualified pet sitter or boarding kennel may be the answer.

Realizing that modern dog owners expect and demand more for their cherished canine companions, many boarding kennels now offer larger, fenced play areas, soft bedding, a variety of toys, specialized feeding programs, professional grooming, pet photography, and pet massage services. Some have gotten into the doggy day care business to provide short-term care to meet the needs of working dog owners, and others have gone so far as to provide rooms instead of kennels, complete with furniture, piped-in music, and other comforts of home for their canine guests.

Evaluating a boarding kennel involves finding out what services are available and physically inspecting the facility to see if it meets your needs. Kennels, runs, and play areas should be clean, well maintained, and free of hazards. Soft bedding and fresh water should be available at all times. The staff should be knowledgeable in the care and handling of dogs, and they should show an interest in the well-being of your pet.

Doggy Day Care

The proliferation of dual-income households has created a new generation of "home alone" dogs. If you are a working pet parent, you may find it difficult to provide enough exercise and socialization for your dog, a need that can be met by the burgeoning population of doggy day care centers. Operating much like a child care center, you can drop your dog off at a doggy day care on your way to work in the morning and pick him up at the end of the work day.

While at doggy day care, your dog will receive plenty of group play time with other dogs, as well as a rest period. Services at the facility might include snacks, grooming, training, or canine massage. Play equipment might include opportunities for climbing, wading in water, or free choice of toys. You do not need to utilize these services on a daily basis, but regularly scheduled visits as infrequent as once a week or a couple times per month may qualify you for discounts.

It may sound like an ideal situation for the busy owner of an energetic Doberman, but doggy day cares are not for every dog. Dogs must be screened for suitable temperament and meet certain health requirements before being allowed to participate. A well-socialized Doberman may indeed find the experience exciting and invigorating, but if he is not accustomed to a noisy and sometimes overstimulating environment, he may become stressed. This is why it is best to start this type of care when your dog is young, or after he has had some experience with group play times with other dogs.

Doggy day cares are not all created equal, so it is important to scrutinize them as carefully as any other pet care service. The ratio of staff to dogs should not exceed 10 to 12 dogs per person so that the animals can be adequately supervised. Safety precautions should include a time-out area to separate dogs if any one of them plays too rough and specially designed entryways to prevent the escape of dogs. Observing the doggy day care while it is in operation is the best way to determine the quality of care provided.

TRAVELING WITH YOUR DOG

If you are like most dog owners, you probably prefer to take your dog with you on trips rather than leaving him in the care of a pet sitter. Following some health, safety, and etiquette guidelines, along with planning in advance and knowing what is expected at your destination, can help make your traveling experience pleasurable for both you and your furry traveling partner.

Preparation

When traveling with your dog, bring along everything he will need while he's away, both to provide for his comfort and to prevent problem behaviors caused by travel issues. Stick to his regular routine as closely as possible. He will not become anxious or stressed if dinner time and play time still occur at their usual times. Set aside time each day to give him extra attention. The more he feels "at home" while traveling, the more relaxed he'll be.

- Before traveling, make sure your dog is healthy and up to date on vaccinations. If you will be traveling to an area with an increased risk of exposure to Lyme disease or heartworm, you may want to obtain additional vaccinations or preventives.
- Prevent nervousness or carsickness by taking your dog on short trips around town so he can learn to be comfortable in a vehicle as well as traveling in a crate or a doggy seatbelt, which are

What to Do If Your Dog Becomes Lost

In the event that your dog becomes lost, acting immediately will increase the chances that you will find him as quickly as possible. Here are just a few things you can do:

- Thoroughly search the area in which your dog was last seen. Lost pets sometimes become confused and frightened, so check under vehicles, beneath bushes, inside sheds, or any other place your dog might decide to hide.

- Call your dog with a special word like "treat," which might entice him to come to you. A favorite toy might also work.

- Check with neighbors in case they have seen your dog, and leave a description of him and your phone number with them.

- Call local shelters, Doberman rescue groups, and government agencies responsible for animal control. Most shelters are only required to hold lost pets for 72 hours before placing them for adoption, so contact them at least every other day. Include all shelters and agencies within a 20-mile radius.

- Make flyers with photos and a description of your dog to distribute to neighbors, veterinarians, groomers, trainers, and pet stores. You can also post flyers on public bulletin boards located in places such as banks, grocery stores, coffee shops, etc. Include your phone number and reward information if desired, but avoid putting your name and address on flyers—some heartless scam artists can use this information to take advantage of you.

- Place an ad in local newspapers. Some are willing to publish lost pet ads for free! Also check the lost and found ads frequently. Always withhold some piece of identifying information so you can screen the leads you receive.

required for his safety at all times.

- Bring a supply of your dog's regular food. A change in diet can cause diarrhea and stress. It is also a good idea to pack some bottled water because some dogs may refuse to drink regional water that smells or tastes different.

- Don't forget to bring your dog's brushes to help keep him free of dirt or plant matter that can make him uncomfortable.

- Make sure your dog receives frequent breaks to relieve himself and stretch his legs, and offer him a drink of water occasionally while traveling.

Safety

You've made all the necessary preparations and arrangements, and you're ready to hit the road. As you embark on your journey, remember that your canine companion's safety is of the utmost importance. Contain your dog in a safe and secure place at all times—whether on the road or in your lodgings.

- One of the most frightening aspects of traveling with your dog is the possibility that he may become lost. Always keep a collar with identification tags on him and make sure your microchip registration is up to date.
- Bring a recent photo of your dog, and keep your veterinarian's number handy for emergencies.
- A small first-aid kit can be a lifesaver when traveling, especially if you enjoy camping.
- Do not leave your dog unattended in a closed vehicle while traveling, especially in warmer climates. If you must leave him in the car for a very short period of time, make sure there is plenty of ventilation by keeping the vehicle windows open and using a battery-operated fan to aid with air circulation.
- Do not let your dog travel with his head out the vehicle window because this can cause eye and ear injuries.

Etiquette

During your travels, and certainly when you arrive at your destination, practice good manners:

- To ensure that pet-friendly vacation spots remain that way, and to avoid complaints and problems with other vacationers, please be vigilant in cleaning up after your dog! Dog doo bags are very compact and can be kept in your car, pocket, or purse to clean up any unexpected messes.
- Pack a supply of treats, dog toys, chews, and other items to keep your dog busy and happy. Bored, destructive, or barking dogs can cause problems for you and other guests.
- Keep your dog leashed. Regardless of how friendly and well trained your dog is, there are always those who are fearful of dogs or have little appreciation for them. Always be respectful of others.

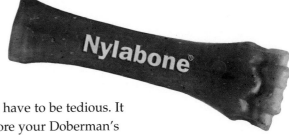

Preparing for your new best friend doesn't have to be tedious. It is a great way to channel your excitement before your Doberman's arrival. Like planning for a vacation, advance preparations obviously help you avoid unexpected surprises, but they also remind you of what is to come and heighten your anticipation. So when the big day comes, everything will culminate in a joyous homecoming for your special dog. Savor that moment!

Chapter

4

FEEDING

Your Doberman Pinscher

eeding a dog is not as simple as it was in the past, when most dog owners piled any unwanted table scraps into a bowl and left them on the floor for the dog. Prior to World War II, dogs were considered scavengers who could easily subsist on human leftovers, but such a diet cost our canine friends dearly in poor health and dental problems.

Commercially packaged dog foods did not initially emerge as a healthy alternative, but rather as a profitable way to dispose of scraps left over from the processing of human food. These foods were no more nutritious than the scraps gleaned straight off the table, but their convenience was attractive enough to gain substantial economic support. Yet this profitability may be responsible for the healthy advancements in commercially prepared foods we (and our dogs) enjoy today.

COMMERCIAL DOG FOODS

The options available in prepackaged dog foods have become so specialized and diverse that it is often difficult to determine which food to purchase. But a few guidelines can help narrow your choices and make this decision process a little easier.

Commercially packaged dog food comes in three different forms: dry, moist, and canned. Although canned and moist foods are more palatable for dogs, they are not very practical to use as a primary meal base. They are expensive, and they tend to stick to the teeth and cause dental problems. Moist foods, in particular, contain a high amount of sugar and additives.

For these reasons, canned and moist foods are most often used as a supplement to dry foods. They are great for stimulating appetite and putting some variety into a dog's diet—could you imagine eating cereal for every single meal? They do provide an opportunity to offer your dog different textures and tastes that will encourage him to eat his meals heartily.

The quality of dry foods varies considerably, and this can have an impact on your dog's general health. The only way to weed out substandard foods from quality ones is to read the package labels. Investigating different dog foods does take a little bit of effort, but it can have a dramatic effect on the health and condition of your dog. Knowing exactly what to

A well-balanced, nutritious diet will help your dog look and feel his best.

look for can help streamline your efforts.

Ingredients

A high-quality food will use meat as a source of protein rather than soy or grain products. Many foods use a combination of protein sources, which is fine, but meat should be the main source of protein (this is indicated by its placement at the top of the ingredients list). The type of meat product used is also an indication of quality because meats listed simply as chicken or beef are superior to meats processed as meal or by-products.

The source of fatty acids used is also important to consider because this contributes to your dog's healthy skin and coat condition. Sources of omega-3 and omega-6 fatty acids are necessary to promote oil production and healthy hair growth, which can have a huge impact on his appearance.

Good sources of fatty acids are fish meal, fish oil, and flaxseed oil, while inferior sources are animal fat and beef tallow. Animal fat is a generic term for fat that is obtained from unspecified sources. It may consist of fat and grease recycled from restaurant operations or food-processing facilities. Beef tallow is a by-product of human food processing that, like animal fat, has a low concentration of linoleic acid, which is important for skin and coat health.

Most dry dog foods are supplemented with vitamins to make them nutritionally complete, but some vitamins have little value if they are not combined with the appropriate supplements to facilitate their absorption into the body. An example of this is vitamin D, which requires a biotin supplement to be of any value. Look for biotin on the ingredients list.

Dry dog foods necessarily require some form of preservative to keep them fresh. While artificial preservatives such as ethoxyquin, butylated hydroxytoluene (BHT), and butylated hydroxyanisole (BHA) have traditionally been used, questions have been raised concerning their affect on health. Many dog food manufacturers have now embraced the trend toward natural forms of preservative, such as vitamins E and C. These are sometimes listed in the ingredients as mixed tocopherols. Although not as effective as artificial preservatives because they do not provide as long a shelf life, wouldn't you take advantage of eliminating artificial additives in your dog's diet if you could?

Guaranteed Analysis Chart

Label information should include a Guaranteed Analysis Chart, which lists the percentage of each nutritional component in the dog food. The two most important elements to check on the chart are the protein and fat content levels. These will indicate whether a food falls under one of several categories: performance, super premium, premium, maintenance, or economy foods.

Performance Foods

Performance foods will have exceptionally high protein and fat levels, up to 32 percent and 20 percent, respectively. These foods are designed for dogs who burn a considerable amount of calories under adverse working conditions. Sled dogs and racing dogs are good candidates for this type of food, but it is not appropriate for the majority of dogs who will quickly gain a ton of unwanted weight.

Super Premium Foods

Super premium foods are also higher in protein and fat levels than most dog foods, averaging around 25 percent protein and 14 percent fat. Again, the additional calories can cause weight gain for most dogs, but they are great for working dogs, performance dogs, or show dogs who require the extra energy boost.

Evaluating Dog Foods

Check dog food labels for the following:

Ingredients: Meat should be the first ingredient listed. Solid meat products are preferable to by-products and meals.

Preservatives: Tocopherols (natural vitamin E or vitamin C preservatives) are preferable to artificial preservatives, such as ethoxyquin, butylated hydroxytoluene (BHT), or butylated hydroxyanisole (BHA).

Fatty Acids: Good sources of fatty acids include fish meal, fish oil, or flaxseed oil. Inferior sources are animal fat and beef tallow.

Rating: The package should state, "Formulated to meet the Association of American Feed Control Officials (AAFCO) Dog Food Nutrient Profile."

Guaranteed Analysis Chart: Premium versions of dry dog foods will boast at least 17 to 23 percent protein and 10 to 12 percent fat content.

Dry dog foods compose the most popular meal base for dogs.

Premium and Maintenance Foods

Premium and maintenance foods are the most commonly used diets. They provide adequate sustenance for dogs in most situations. With protein levels between 17 and 25 percent, and fat content between 10 and 14 percent, they meet the basic requirements for dogs under average exercise and environmental conditions. The difference between premium and maintenance foods is that premium foods tend to consist of better quality ingredients.

Premium foods also cost more, of course, but better ingredients means easier digestion and efficient utilization of the food, which results in less food being needed to maintain weight and good condition. By requiring less amounts of food, the price difference between premium and maintenance foods becomes negligible.

The difference you will notice most when upgrading from a maintenance diet to a premium diet is an improvement in your dog's general condition and appearance: a glossier coat, more energy and enthusiasm, and solid muscle development. These characteristics are absolutely essential if you plan to show or exhibit your dog. Maintenance diets, however, remain a good alternative for dogs who tend to gain too much weight on premium diets.

Economy Foods

Economy foods are those that meet the bare essentials for a complete and balanced canine diet. Containing inferior ingredients and low levels of protein and fat, they often include fillers such as corn, corn meal, soy beans, and peanut hulls that provide little if any nutritional value. Fillers are not easily digested or absorbed by the body and pass right through, so it takes a larger amount of food to maintain weight. What appears to be an economic value really is not, because like everything else in life, you get what you pay for.

AAFCO Approval

The Association of American Feed Control Officials (AAFCO) sets minimum standards of nutrition for dog food manufacturers. If the commercially prepared dog food meets these standards, the package will state, "Formulated to meet the AAFCO Dog Food Nutrient Profile." But keep in mind that these are *minimum* standards, and they do not guarantee quality ingredients. It does certify that the food will provide the appropriate components for proper tissue growth and maintenance so that health problems due to nutritional deficiencies can be avoided.

HOME-COOKED DOG FOODS

As advanced as the production of commercially prepared dog foods has become, there are still problems in assessing the quality of these foods and their affect on health. Ingredient lists do not specify the source of the ingredients, which bears directly on ingredient quality. Then there are those long, technical names for ingredients, but most people have no idea what they are or how safe they are. And of course, additives to enhance color, texture, and flavor are always a concern.

Distrustful of the safety and nutritional value of commercial foods, some dog owners have resorted to cooking their dogs' meals themselves. Home-cooked dog foods are an excellent option if your dog suffers from digestive problems or allergies from commercially prepared foods because they give you complete control over what your dog is consuming.

Often consisting of cooked meats and hard-boiled eggs for protein, cottage cheese for calcium, pasta or rice for carbohydrates, and vegetables for a variety of vitamins, the hardest part of creating home-cooked meals is developing the right combination of ingredients in the right proportions to be nutritionally complete. For this reason, you need to research this option thoroughly, analyze recipes for nutrition, and contact your veterinarian for advice before implementing this type of diet. In most cases, vitamins and supplements need to be added to ensure the diet has no deficiencies.

Setting aside the time necessary for preparation is another issue to consider. You can prepare meals a week in advance by refrigerating or freezing unused portions, but you must have the correct ingredients on hand and a specific time period each week to assemble and store the meals. Substituting ingredients or switching to a commercially prepared food when time does not permit preparation of home-cooked meals can cause digestive upset for your dog.

Commercial pet food manufacturers have not ignored the trend of natural, healthier diets for dogs, and there are now prepackaged

Home-Cooked Food Caution

Some people subscribe to the mistaken notion that home-cooked dog food is the same as table scraps. After all, home-cooked dog food basically contains the same ingredients we prepare for our own meals, right? So why not pile meats, vegetables, and breads from your dinner into your dog's dish? While it's true that people food is perfectly edible for dogs, the types and proportions of foods fed must be carefully calculated, and vitamins and minerals added, to make them nutritionally complete because a dog's nutritional needs are very different from those of a human. Contact your veterinarian for advice before implementing this type of diet.

forms of home-cooked foods available. These dry or canned foods are very high in protein levels, contain little if any grain products, and consist of familiar ingredients like turkey, chicken, carrots, potatoes, eggs, and cottage cheese. Commercial versions of home-cooked food certainly provide more convenience than preparing the food yourself, but you can expect a considerably higher price tag for this type of food.

A carefully designed home-cooked diet can have many advantages for dogs with special needs. Check with your vet to make sure that this type of diet is right for your Doberman.

RAW FOOD DIETS

The Bones and Raw Food (BARF) Diet became popular in the 1990s with the publication of Ian Billinghurst's book, *Give Your Dog a Bone*. At first considered a fad, it has gained the loyalty and advocacy of many. Touted as the most natural canine diet available, it involves feeding raw meat and bone products that more closely resemble what dogs would consume in the wild. Those who practice this type of canine nutritional management know that the heating process involved in producing commercially prepared or home-cooked dog foods strips the food of valuable nutrients.

But there are also those who point out the shortcomings of this type of diet. The Federal Drug Administration (FDA), veterinarians, and other experts warn of the dangers of consuming bone products that can potentially cause internal damage. There is also a risk posed by parasites and bacteria often harbored in raw meat products. Some even claim the BARF diet does not accurately represent a naturally balanced diet because it lacks the entrails and other tissues normally consumed in the wild.

A raw diet may consist of chicken wings, chicken backs, raw eggs, beef liver, or fish as a main source of protein, and it will often be rounded out with raw vegetables, grain products, and vitamins to make it nutritionally complete. Because bacteria can multiply rapidly in raw meat, this type of diet cannot be prepared in advance, so ingredients must not be combined more than three days prior to feeding. Unused portions need to be kept refrigerated.

A raw food diet does require a time commitment and will have an impact on your pocketbook because it is considerably more expensive than commercially prepared dog food.

Considering all the pros and cons of the BARF diet can help you determine if it is right for you and your dog. Advocates credit the diet with producing a stronger immune system and reducing the risk of disease, benefits that are yet unproven scientifically but are supported by numerous testimonials. Researching this diet thoroughly prior to implementing it is the key to avoiding problems.

Of course, like anything else that experiences a surge in popularity, the BARF diet has found a niche in commercial production as well. Called "Biologically Appropriate Raw Food," prepackaged versions of this diet are now available as frozen patties distributed by a network of vendors. They can be found through natural pet food outlets, breeders, and trainers. Adding convenience and balanced nutrition is likely to make the commercial BARF diet preferable to manual preparation, but like any other type of commercially prepared dog food,

Vitamins	
A	Affects hearing, vision, digestion, nerves, and muscle coordination
B complex	This group of vitamins requires interaction among all members of the complex to work, so they are often given in a combined unit containing the following B vitamins:
B-1 (Thiamine)	Aids appetite and muscle function
B-2 (Riboflavin)	Assists with growth, food absorption, red blood cell production, and antibody production
B-3 (Niacin)	Helps the circulatory and nervous systems
B-5 (Pantothenic acid)	Affects the adrenal gland functions and supports the immune and digestive systems
B-6 (Pyridoxine)	Helps the body metabolize protein and affects the nervous and immune systems
B-9 (Folic acid)	Assists with protein metabolism and red blood cell production, and also affects the immune and reproductive systems
B-12 (Cobalamin)	Affects growth, fertility, and digestion
Biotin	Necessary to utilize fats for healthy skin and also supports the endocrine, reproductive, and nervous systems
D	Regulates calcium and phosphorus to produce healthy bones and teeth
E	Affects the circulatory, reproductive, and immune systems; known as an antioxidant, it helps oxygenate and purify the blood, and also helps heal damaged skin

you should analyze the ingredients, percentage charts, feeding recommendations, and handling instructions.

SPECIAL DIETS

Food is a necessary fuel for the body, but it also provides treatment options for a number of health conditions. Dogs with kidney, liver, or heart failure can experience greater longevity and better quality of life through the use of special diets. Special diets can also help manage diabetes, urinary problems, allergies, and obesity in dogs by reducing certain dietary components that aggravate these conditions and increasing the nutrients and vitamins that help combat them.

Because you are probably not a canine nutritional expert, and you probably don't have any desire to become one, it's a good thing that most special diets are available only through veterinary prescription. Proper diagnosis of a condition must be made before a successful diet plan can be implemented. Improper use of special diets may compound an existing condition or cause new problems to develop. Always consult with your veterinarian if you think your dog may need a special diet.

VITAMINS AND SUPPLEMENTS

Most dogs do quite well on a quality commercial dog food that meets the requirements of a complete and balanced diet. Vitamins and supplements are already added to commercially prepared dog foods to make sure they meet the nutritional needs for most dogs. But *most dogs* does not mean *all dogs*. Veterinarians and other experts are beginning to realize that nutritional needs vary from one dog to another and can be quite different for individual breeds. The long-haired Samoyed, for instance, obviously requires more protein to maintain his thick, arctic coat, while the Doberman may require more calories to meet his demand for energy. Certain life stages and physical conditions may also indicate a need for dietary supplementation.

General-Purpose Multivitamins

General-purpose multivitamins, which are available through most pet supply outlets, are designed to meet a broad spectrum of needs and can benefit just about any dog. They can compensate for any nutritional deficiencies in your dog's typical fare. Your dog can

Minerals	
Calcium	Needed for bones, teeth, blood, muscles, and nerves
Phosphorus	Needed for bones, teeth, and blood, but also helps metabolize carbohydrates and fats
Iron	Crucial for red blood cell production, which affects energy and immunity
Copper	Works with iron to form hemoglobin (red blood cells)
Potassium	Necessary to regulate blood and assists with muscle function
Sodium	Helps regulate body fluids
Selenium	An antioxidant that helps regulate blood sugar and can affect immunity, muscles, skin, and fertility
Iodine	Necessary for thyroid health and also affects metabolism
Magnesium	Supports the heart, bones, muscles, and nervous system
Manganese	Necessary for the body to utilize enzymes and affects reproductive functions, bone and cartilage growth, pituitary gland function, and nervous and immune system health

experience greater immunity to disease, higher energy levels, better digestion and circulation, and a noticeable improvement in skin and coat condition. But perhaps the greatest benefit is simply the peace of mind they can give you. You won't need to guess whether your dog is getting all the vitamins he needs.

Life-Stage Multivitamins

Multivitamins are also designed to meet the specific needs of different life stages. They can be particularly beneficial for puppies, pregnant or lactating females, and aged dogs. During these life stages, adequate nutrition is especially important. Multivitamins designed to meet the nutritional needs of puppies contain higher levels of vitamins and minerals needed for bone and tissue growth. Pregnant females can benefit from a general-purpose multivitamin or one recommended for stressed or active dogs (to meet the additional demands on their bodies). Multivitamins for senior dogs often include higher levels of vitamins and minerals to help with skin and coat condition, appetite stimulation, and joint flexibility.

Individual Vitamins

Individual vitamins are also available to meet any specific dietary need, but these are most often used at a veterinarian's recommendation when a specific health condition calls for their use. Vitamin E may be prescribed for a dog suffering from skin damage to help the skin rejuvenate. Vitamin C can help strengthen the immunity of a sick dog. But individual vitamins should not be used indiscriminately. Too much of any one vitamin may do more harm than good, so consult with your veterinarian for advice and dosage information before supplementing your dog's diet with individual vitamins.

Supplements

Supplements are similar to multivitamins in that they provide extra dietary components to aid health. But instead of having a general purpose, they are usually formulated to provide specific health benefits. Dogs with arthritis can find relief with supplements containing glucosamine and chondroitin. Dogs with allergies can enjoy healthier skin with supplements that provide omega-3 and omega-6 fatty acids. Supplements can also strengthen immunities and help with urinary tract or digestive problems. They are now widely available through most pet supply sources.

FEEDING A PUPPY

Your new puppy will undoubtedly find adjusting to a new home somewhat stressful. He may miss his mother or littermates, and there will be many new rules to learn. A change in diet at this time may compound the stress and cause digestive upset and diarrhea. So if you know what type of food your puppy received before you brought him home, it is best to keep him on the same diet for at least a couple of weeks until things settle down. This will give you a chance to research various dog foods before making a firm

Feeding Schedule for Your Doberman Pinscher

Age	Feeding Recommendations
0 to 8 wks	Puppies at this age need their mother's milk for adequate nutrition and to help them develop immunities. They can begin transitioning to soft dog foods at five or six weeks old. Dry puppy foods can be introduced at six to eight weeks of age.
8 to 12 wks	Most puppies are weaned from their mothers between eight and ten weeks old. Until they are three months old, they should be fed at least three times per day.
12 wks to 1 yr	Twice daily feedings can begin at 12 weeks of age and continue throughout your dog's adulthood. Puppies can be transitioned to an adult version of dog food between 10 and 12 months of age.

commitment to the food of your choice.

Whatever food you eventually choose to use, it should be appropriate for the current life stage of your dog. Doberman puppies experience a lot of growth the first year, and they need the higher levels of nutrients and calories found in puppy food. Your Doberman pup should be fed a good-quality puppy food until he is between 10 and 12 months of age.

Your dog's nutritional requirements are determined by age; puppies will have different needs than adults or seniors.

Changing Foods

Because an abrupt change in diet can be stressful to the system, any change should be made gradually. Whether you are changing from one brand of commercial dog food to another, or switching to a home-prepared diet, it helps to mix a little of the new food with your puppy's old diet to help his system adjust. By gradually increasing the portion of new food while reducing the amount of old food over a period of one to two weeks, you can prevent problems with diarrhea that can cause your dog distress and complicate housetraining efforts.

How Much and How Often to Feed

How much and how often to feed depends on your puppy's age, size, growth spurts, energy spurts, and individual metabolism. Puppies between 8 and 12 weeks old should be fed at least three times per day, while puppies over 12 weeks old can be reduced to twice-daily feedings. The quantity of food to supply at each of these feedings is a little more complicated to calculate because your puppy's needs are constantly changing, but the feeding instructions on commercial dog food packages are a good place to start.

Refer to the recommended feeding schedule on the package and then adjust the amount according to your observations. If your puppy finishes his meal within 10 minutes and still appears to be hungry for more, increase the amount of food until he appears satiated. If your puppy walks away from his meal when there is

Healthy feeding practices combined with daily exercise can keep your dog from becoming overweight.

causing a bloated appearance to the belly and extreme pain. Bloat can often result in death within 24 hours if veterinary treatment is not obtained immediately.

The Benefits of Feeding Twice Per Day

In addition to preventing bloat, feeding twice per day has benefits if you work full time and have to leave your dog home alone during the day. Eating is a stimulant for bowel movements, so providing a feeding and an adequate potty break for your dog in the morning before you leave for work can help reduce the chance of household accidents during the day. This is preferable to leaving your dog hungry all day because a hungry, bored dog is more prone to get into trouble when left alone. Another feeding in the evening will have the same effect on elimination patterns and help prevent nighttime accidents.

Feed Your Dog First

Although some sources recommend feeding a dog *after* his humans have enjoyed their own meal—the purpose of which is to supposedly enforce human superiority by having people eat first— it is a practice that will undoubtedly contribute to vigilant, pleading eyes beside your dinner table. You cannot expect a hungry dog not to be tempted by the scent of human food! So feed your dog first and reduce his temptation to beg.

Feeding your dog first will also reduce your temptation to enhance his meal with human leftovers. Adding dinner scraps to your dog's meal destroys the balanced nutrition of his dog food, can lead to unwanted weight gain, and can also create a finicky eater. A healthy rule to remember is: People food is for people, and dog food is for dogs.

FEEDING AN OLDER DOG

When your Doberman Pinscher reaches the age of seven, you may notice some signs of aging. He may become less active and sleep more often. He may show signs of joint stiffness, poor skin and coat condition, or reduced vision and hearing. He may also develop certain conditions common in aging pets, such as decreased liver and kidney function, circulatory problems, or dental problems.

Many of the conditions accepted as inevitable signs of aging can be managed with special diets, vitamins, or supplements. The most common special diet for older dogs is dog food specially formulated to contain fewer calories and less protein and fat. Weight gain is unavoidable when an older dog continues to consume the same amount of calories as he did when he was younger and more active. Excess weight can, in turn, aggravate other age-related conditions by putting additional stress on joints and internal organs.

Dobermans are active dogs, and as such, many do well on an adult maintenance diet well into their senior years. But signs of weight gain are an obvious indication that a diet change may be necessary. Senior diets help provide the bulk necessary to keep your dog feeling satiated while eliminating the calories he doesn't need. Choosing a quality senior diet involves analyzing the ingredients and guaranteed analysis chart on the package, just as you would when choosing any other type of prepackaged dog food.

Obesity-Related Conditions

- cancer
- congestive heart failure
- dental problems
- diabetes
- heat intolerance
- high blood pressure
- joint and spine problems
- reduced liver function
- respiratory disease
- skin problems

FEEDING PROBLEMS

If there is anything in life that excites a dog, it is food. There's no doubt that dogs love to eat, and there are some Dobermans who think eating is the whole purpose of living! Of course, if you love your dog, you find immense pleasure in making him happy. But using treats, human tidbits, and consumable bones to show just how much you care is not in your or your dog's best interest.

Obesity, begging, finicky eating, and food stealing are all problems that can result from improper food management. Although an occasional treat certainly causes no harm, if you want to see that special spark of happiness in your dog's eyes, give him some attention and play time instead. Your bond will grow stronger, and your dog will be healthier.

Obesity

When one of your guests playfully calls your dog "Tubby" when his real name is "Peppy," you may suddenly realize that, yes, your dog has gotten a little chunky. Right before your eyes, he has gained 10 pounds (4.5 kg), and you wonder how this could have happened. But the process of becoming obese is so gradual that it can easily escape your notice if you are not on the constant lookout for it.

If your dog is a little heavier than he should be, he has a lot of company in the Obese Dog Club. It is estimated that up to 40 percent of companion dogs are overweight. Canine obesity has become a serious concern for dogs in both the United States and Great Britain. Popularity aside, this is not a club of which you want your dog to be a member. Obesity causes more health problems than any other physical condition because it affects virtually every system of the body. Accumulation of fat diminishes the effectiveness of internal organs including the heart, liver, and lungs. It places a damaging burden on joints and aggravates arthritis. And to make matters worse, it increases the risk of cancer by 50 percent.

Checking Your Dog's Weight

The easiest way to prevent this condition is to be observant and follow healthy feeding practices. You have an advantage in monitoring your dog's weight because your Doberman has a short, sleek coat that cannot conceal a barrel-shaped body or protruding ribs like the coat of a longhaired dog could.

You can check your dog's weight occasionally while petting or grooming him. You should be able to feel his ribs, but they should be softened with a moderate layer of protective fat. If you cannot easily feel his ribs, alas, your dog has tipped the scales at chubby. If his ribs or hipbones are visually noticeable, or they can be felt easily, he is underweight.

Preventing Obesity

Healthy feeding practices include limiting treats, keeping table scraps out of your dog's meals, and forbidding the feeding of morsels from the dinner table. A regular period of exercise each day will also help keep your dog fit and trim. If you use food rewards in training, choose treats that are lower in calories and fat, and limit training sessions so that your dog's diet does not become unbalanced by the consumption of too many training treats.

Treatment for Obesity

Prevention is always preferable to a cure, but once you have recognized that your dog has a weight problem, it is important to take steps to correct it. If he is slightly overweight, this is a matter of simply reducing the amount you feed him and providing a little more exercise. If he has a more serious weight issue, veterinarian advice is recommended.

Specialty diets are available to help in a weight loss program, and your veterinarian is the best one to suggest the right diet for your dog. If your dog has developed any health conditions related to obesity, this can be considered in devising an appropriate diet and exercise plan.

Finicky Eaters

Feeding people food to dogs is the leading contributor to obesity, but it also encourages the development of other eating problems. Dogs who become accustomed to having their meals touched up with table scraps or other enhancements are likely to become finicky eaters. Fortunately, Dobermans are known to have robust appetites to fuel their energy needs, so finicky eating is generally not as serious a problem for them as it is for some other breeds.

Preventing and Correcting Finicky Eating

Again, by avoiding the habit of enhancing your dog's meals, you can prevent finicky eating habits. But once the problem has developed, it must be corrected. If your dog has a particularly difficult time adjusting to nonembellished meals, you may have to wean him off them gradually or replace the additions to his meals with something palatable but more appropriate, such as canned or moist dog foods. Motivating a fussy Doberman to eat usually entails no more than a slight stimulation of his appetite. Once his salivary glands begin to churn, he is likely to demolish the rest of his meal in short order.

Begging

Begging is yet another feeding problem caused by sharing human food with our canine companions. Its roots may be based

Are You Training Your Dog to Beg?

Using people food as rewards during training will not encourage your dog to beg as long as you are not consuming his treats while training him. Dogs love people food, but it is not the food that creates a beggar—it is the act of *sharing* food with your dog (handing food to your dog while eating it yourself).

There is always more than one way to teach your dog to do any one skill, and it is better to use training methods that do not require you to tease your dog by eating his treats in front of him or putting his treats in your mouth to gain his attention (an attention exercise used in some dog training classes). Can you think of any better way to teach your dog to beg than by encouraging him to look at you when you have food in your mouth?

Remember the rule: People food is for people, and dog food (even if it is human food used as dog treats) is for dogs.

on survival instincts that are as natural as the desire to pursue game or curl up in a warm ball to sleep, which could explain why this behavior develops so easily and why it is so common. Just one tidbit from the dinner table is enough to inspire a vigilantly begging dog who persistently pesters diners.

Preventing and Correcting Begging

Preventing and correcting this behavior is a matter of adopting a strict rule forbidding the sharing of people food with your dog. This is not restricted only to meal times, but also applies at any time people are consuming food. Most dogs will soon learn to accept that handouts will not be forthcoming, and they will resign themselves to lying quietly under the dinner table to snuffle up dropped crumbs (which are perfectly fair game).

It is a good practice to completely ignore your dog during your meals. Don't pet him, talk to him, or even look at him when you are eating. Temptation to beg is at its height when a dog is hungry, so feeding your dog before meal times or parties will make it easier for him to accept the fact that he will not be partaking with you.

Using the Place Command

Dogs who already have a well-established habit of begging may benefit from being taught the *place* command. Choose a place within sight of your dining area and instruct your dog to lie down there. When he complies, reward him. Gradually increase the amount of time you expect him to hold his position there, and begin using the *place* command. When your dog is consistently obedient to this command, you can use it during mealtimes. Don't forget to reward your dog after dinner for his good behavior because this will continue to reinforce it.

Food Stealing

A dog's strong desire for human food can result in food stealing. This occurs when a dog snatches food from kitchen tables, counters, coffee tables, or even directly from the hands of children or unwary guests. Imagine your disappointment upon returning from firing up the grill to discover your dog has consumed the expensive T-bone steaks you left on the counter! This scenario is not unheard of for Doberman owners because they are large enough to reach food at a higher level than some dogs.

Preventing Food Stealing

The most logical solution to this problem is to keep food out of your dog's reach, especially when you are not present. Food stealers have little self-control when left to their own devices, and food left on the counter is unreasonably tempting. Just as you cannot expect a child to ignore candy left within reach, you cannot expect your Doberman to resist the allure of human food left within his grasp.

Using the Leave It Command

When you are present, your dog can learn to respect that your food is off limits. You can teach the *leave it* command to make this clear to him. This training begins with a small food item used as bait and a tastier treat for a reward. With your dog seated in front of you, hold the bait out in one hand and instruct your dog to *leave it*. If he tries to grab the bait, close your hand to prevent him from getting it. If he pulls away from the bait or ignores it, reward him with the treat (and a lot of praise).

Once your dog understands what *leave it* means, you can progress to more challenging exercises by placing the bait on the floor in front of him and restraining him with a leash if he tries to snatch it. You can use more appealing items for bait to help make him more reliable at this command. And finally, you can place bait in certain locations where you want to teach him to leave food alone, such as the coffee table, dining table, or end table, and walk your dog through the house on a leash to test him. Eventually, your dog will learn that food left in these locations is not meant for him.

The *leave it* command is more than a way to teach your dog household manners; it becomes a safety measure any time he comes into contact with edible items outside the home. Some dogs may try to eat dead animal parts, rotten or moldy food, or even sweet-tasting but deadly antifreeze that has leaked onto the driveway. A dog who has been taught the *leave it* command can be prevented from consuming anything he should not.

Household Manners

The moment your dog comes home, he will begin to learn how to live in your household, whether you intend to teach him or not. Therefore, it is important to establish household rules ahead of time and solicit training participation from all members of the family. Make proper food management part of your training routine by establishing appropriate feeding habits right from the start—your dog will be happier and healthier for it.

FOOD AS MOTIVATION ▰▰▰

Dogs and dolphins don't have a whole lot in common, but there is one characteristic they share: They are both highly motivated by food! Food rewards have been used to train marine mammals for many decades, and they have since been found to be exceptionally motivating in the training of other species as well, including dogs and horses. With a strong motivator like food, dogs can be trained quicker and easier with minimal use of corrections, so it's not surprising that most dog trainers now use food rewards as a valuable tool.

However, while food rewards may make the process of training easier for you and obviously more enjoyable for your dog, they also pose some problems. Feeding your dog too many treats can undermine the best diet plan, and some treats can create havoc with your dog's digestive system.

Preventing Problems With Food-Reward Training

To prevent problems with food-reward training, it is important to choose the right treats. Pure meat products are better than processed meats like lunchmeats, hot dogs, and sausages, which contain high levels of salt, additives, and preservatives. Cheese is a dairy product that is difficult for some dogs to digest, and it is notorious for causing diarrhea.

Many healthy, low-calorie dog treats are now available on the market, and these are a good alternative. Another healthy option is homemade treats because these give you complete control over the ingredients your dog is consuming. Soft, chewy ones are the most desirable, and dogs love the freshness and natural ingredients!

Limiting Treats

Measuring and limiting the amount of treats used during training sessions can help prevent unbalancing your dog's diet. Treats are great facilitators for rapid learning, but they do not necessarily need to be used after a dog has already learned a skill. Expect your dog to perform some basic skills like *sit, stay,* or *down* without compensation, and replace food rewards with other types of rewards, such as praise, toys, or playtime, whenever possible.

"Jackpotting" is a dog training term for rewarding a correct behavior with a large amount of treats, the purpose of which is to make it exceptionally clear to your dog that he has performed correctly. Avoid jackpotting unless your dog is having considerable difficulty learning a new skill. In most cases, jackpotting can be replaced with a little more time and patience. Treats, especially those that are high in fat and calories, should be used sparingly during training unless you want your dog to become a gratuitous member of the Obese Dog Club.

FOODS TO AVOID

Dogs have subsisted on the scraps of human food for thousands of years. But just because a food is edible to humans doesn't mean it's safe for dogs. Some human foods can cause serious toxic reactions or other complications in dogs! The following food items should be kept out of reach of your dog:

- chocolate
- coffee and tea
- grapes and raisins
- hops (used in brewing)
  - leaves of tomatoes, potatoes, and rhubarb
- macadamia nuts
- moldy foods
- nutmeg
- onions
- seeds of fruits
- yeast dough

If you think your dog is having a reaction to ingesting any of these items, contact your veterinarian immediately, or call the ASPCA Animal Poison Control Hotline at (888) 426-4435.

Your dog requires food to survive, but he requires *good* food to live a long and happy life. Sure, your Doberman will probably eat just about anything you put in front of him, but why not make it something that will help to keep him healthy, reduce your veterinary expenses, and give him several extra years to spend by your side? Take pride in your dog and care for him as you would any other prized possession. His thanks will be expressed in his bright eyes and his enthusiasm for life.

GROOMING

Your Doberman Pinscher

As smooth as silk and as shiny as a new Corvette, the Doberman's million-dollar coat catches the eye of anyone who appreciates the finer things in life! But this sleek and attractive packaging has a lot of practical appeal as well. The Doberman's short, glossy coat requires little maintenance and makes him an exceptionally clean housedog.

Unlike those breeds with a thick, fluffy undercoat, his hair doesn't shed out in clumps and cling like cat claws to every piece of clothing and furniture. There are no giant dust bunnies rolling like tumbleweeds throughout the house from this trim canine! He is indeed a housekeeper's dream. But low maintenance does not mean no maintenance.

There is no doubt that a well-groomed Doberman is the epitome of beauty and elegance, and it doesn't take much effort to achieve such perfection. However, grooming is more than tending to a dog's outward beauty. It is a health maintenance routine that can prevent oral, ocular, eye, or lameness problems. It can assist with early detection of health conditions such as tumors, arthritis, or skin infections. And most enjoyably, grooming provides one of the most pleasurable bonding opportunities for you and your dog.

GROOMING AS A HEALTH CHECK

A thorough grooming gives you the opportunity to check your dog's body from head to tail, literally. Your dog's nose should be checked for any discharge, his mouth should be examined for teeth and gum problems, and his eyes should be watched for excessive tearing, squinting, or cloudiness in the lens. Your dog's ears should be checked for redness or swelling, but a good sniff may tell you more than a visual inspection will reveal. The odor of an ear infection is unmistakable, and when caught early enough, it can be treated without veterinary intervention by daily cleaning with a cotton ball lightly saturated with rubbing alcohol. Run your hands over your dog's entire body, including his head, neck, chest, back, belly, legs, feet, and tail. Do you feel any roughness of the skin, or any lumps or bumps?

Regular grooming keeps your canine companion healthy and looking good.

Anything unusual should be brought to your vet's attention. Handling your dog's body in this way is more than a way to detect health problems; it is also great training for your dog. It desensitizes him to being touched, especially in those more sensitive areas. This can make him easier to handle in a variety of situations, especially during veterinary visits and show judge examinations.

Finally, examine your dog's feet and tail. Check the pads of the feet for abrasions, and don't forget to look between the pads as well because objects can easily become imbedded there. The rectum can be a prime location for the development of tumors, especially in older dogs, and it can also show evidence of tapeworms, diarrhea, or other health conditions. Don't be too shy to take a peek under your dog's tail!

Professional dog groomers are always on the alert for signs of health problems, and you can learn how to be just as observant. Because dogs tend to mask pain and discomfort, early detection of problems relies on paying close attention to their physical condition. When done regularly as part of your grooming routine, a health check can prevent a minor problem from becoming more serious. This, in turn, can reduce your veterinary expenses and minimize discomfort for your dog.

BRUSHING

The Doberman's coat doesn't appear to require frequent brushing because it is naturally smooth and shiny. The close-lying hair rarely looks disheveled unless it comes into contact with something wet or sticky, and it is true that a once- or twice-a-month brushing is all that is necessary for minimal maintenance. But if you really want your Doberman to glisten like polished brass and keep him in the peak of health, a weekly brushing can do wonders.

Brushing helps loosen and remove dead skin. It stimulates the production of new skin cells and distributes the oils in the coat to bring out that famous shine. It helps remove dead hair, which tends to bristle out of the coat and tarnish the sleek quality we so admire.

Grooming Tools

Grooming may seem like a simple process for such a low-maintenance dog, but there are some tricks to getting the best results. Using the appropriate tools for your dog's coat type is most important. Because the Doberman has short hair without a protective undercoat, brushes that are too harsh can irritate or damage his skin. A rubber curry brush is necessary to work up the coat to bring out the oils, dead skin, and dead hair. A soft-bristled brush is needed to smooth out the coat and whisk away the dead skin and hair that has been brought to the surface of the coat.

Curry brushes come in all different types. They can be round rubber brushes with or without a handle strap on the back. Some

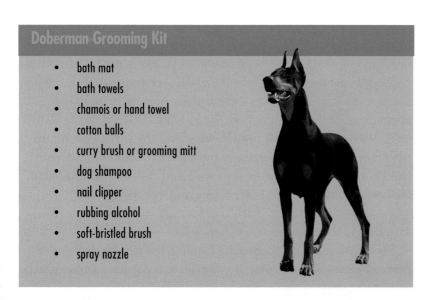

Doberman Grooming Kit

- bath mat
- bath towels
- chamois or hand towel
- cotton balls
- curry brush or grooming mitt
- dog shampoo
- nail clipper
- rubbing alcohol
- soft-bristled brush
- spray nozzle

The Doberman's short, sleek coat is easy to take care of with weekly brushings.

are made of hard rubber and some are made of soft rubber. They might also come in the form of a glove or grooming mitt with rubber or plastic nibs on the palm and fingers. Regardless of whether you choose a curry brush or grooming mitt, soft rubber with short to medium length nibs are best for the Doberman's coat type. Coarser brushes will be too abrasive. When currying your dog, a gentle but firm circular motion will rough up the coat and draw dead skin and hair to the surface of the coat.

After the coat has been roughed up, use the curry brush to smooth out the coat by brushing in the direction the hair naturally lies. Follow up by brushing with a soft-bristled brush in the direction the hair grows. This will help remove the unsightly flakes of skin on the surface of the coat and distribute oils evenly through the hair.

After brushing, your dog will look sleeker and shinier, but there is one more step that makes a miraculous improvement in his appearance. Show dog handlers use a chamois skin (a suede leather cloth often used to polish cars) to wipe over the entire coat (in the direction the hair lies) to achieve the most fabulous shine. A terry cloth hand towel works almost as well, and you will be amazed at the results. Get ready to shield your eyes from the glint!

BATHING

Such clean dogs rarely require bathing, but situations do arise that call for a good washing. If you plan to show your Doberman, baths are an important part of grooming preparation. Your dog may occasionally like to roll in smelly matter to cover up his own scent, and there is always the chance he may, heaven forbid, come into contact with a skunk.

If you use your dog for therapy work or other activities that involve close contact with people, baths can help keep your dog smelling good. They can also minimize hair shedding, which always becomes more pronounced when the hair is worked up from petting and handling. If you allow your dog on the furniture or bed, or if you have young children in the house, cleanliness may be a greater concern.

Where to Bathe Your Doberman

The problem with bathing a Doberman is his size. The bathroom tub can make a suitable wash station when fitted with rubber footing to prevent slipping and to protect the tub from scratches. A hose with a spray head is available at many pet supply outlets and can easily be fitted to the shower pipe. A stationary tub in the basement may also suffice if it is large enough and if it is fitted with a rubber mat and spray hose.

Another option is to rent a bath station at a local boarding or training facility. These often have full-size tubs for bathing as well as blow-drying equipment. And finally, you might consider using the services of a professional pet groomer to do the job. It may be more expensive, but how much are you willing to pay to avoid the mess and hassle? Perhaps dog hair in your tub doesn't appeal to

Get Ready, Get Set, and Then Bathe

Nothing is more frustrating than wetting your dog down in the tub and then realizing you left the shampoo on the kitchen counter. Assemble all your bathing supplies before you put your dog in the tub.

Get Ready: Have your towels, shampoo, cream rinse (if desired), cotton balls (for your dog's ears), and leash organized within easy reach of the tub.

Get Set: Make sure your spray nozzle is attached (if applicable) and the water temperature is adjusted.

Then Bathe: Now you can go get your dog!

you. Maybe you don't like getting as wet as your dog each time you have to bathe him. If having your dog spray water all over your house when he shakes really turns you off, or if you just plain don't have the time, by all means, don't hesitate to contact a professional.

Bathing Tips

Assuming you choose to keep your money in your pocket, bathing your dog at home is a reasonable choice. Washing him doesn't have to be any more complicated than wetting the fur with lukewarm water, working up a good lather of shampoo, and then rinsing it out thoroughly. But you can do a few things to make bathing a little easier on you and your dog.

First, begin by wetting your dog's feet and legs to give him a chance to adjust to the water temperature. Then wet the rest of his body from the belly up and from the rear to the neck. Keep his head dry until you are ready to wash it. This has a distinct advantage because as soon as your dog's ears get wet he will attempt to shake. You can avoid taking a shower during his entire bath if you save his head for last.

After shampooing and thoroughly rinsing the body, begin to wet your dog's head. If you hold his nose down while wetting, it will prevent water from running into it and making him uncomfortable. Avoid getting water into the ears—professional groomers often use cotton balls to keep water out of the ears during baths—because moisture in the ears contributes to the breeding of bacteria that cause ear infections.

Shampoo can be irritating to your dog's eyes, so keep suds away from them and be sure shampoo doesn't run into them when rinsing. When the body and head have both been shampooed and rinsed, squeeze excess water from the coat by running your hands along your dog's body and down his legs (a small rubber squeegee works well for this, too). Then, a quick wrap with a towel will prevent that awful shaking from turning your house into a rain forest.

Numerous dog shampoo products are on the market, and you may want to experiment with them to find those that give the best results. You can also ask groomers or dog show exhibitors which products they prefer. There are color-enhancing shampoos, flea and tick shampoos, tearless shampoos, and shampoos for dogs

If you plan to show your Doberman, baths are an important part of grooming preparation.

with allergies or sensitive skin. Choose a shampoo for your dog's particular needs, but *never* use human shampoos. They are not formulated for a dog's skin and coat type, and can be exceptionally irritating if they get into his eyes.

DRYING

The Doberman's short coat does not have a sponge-like undercoat to soak up and hold moisture, so it dries relatively quickly on its own after a good towel rub and light brushing. Blow drying is generally not necessary unless it is a priority to get your dog dry as quickly as possible. You do not want to let your wet Doberman out in frigid weather, and if you don't like damp spots left on the carpeting where he lies, you can blow dry him with a regular hair dryer on a low setting.

Blow drying can help dry your dog quickly and can also blow out a lot of dead hair during shedding season. The only problem with blow drying a Doberman is that it tends to fluff up the hair and sacrifices some of the sleekness that is the breed's trademark. If you do blow dry your dog, be patient while he gets accustomed to the noise and air force. Never blow directly into your dog's face or ears; these areas are best left to air dry.

GROOMING FOR SHOWING

Show dogs are the super models of the dog world. Many are primped and prepared for hours, days, even weeks before a show to make them look their best. Because the Doberman doesn't require the intense grooming some breeds do, you might think, "Give another hoot for short hair!"

The truth is, you do have to prepare for a show weeks in advance. Thin-haired dogs like Dobermans are exceptionally prone to scratches and scrapes that can blemish their sleek appearance. These must be prevented or treated ahead of time. Hot spots (balding or thinning areas) also need time to be corrected. You also have to be careful how often and how long your dog wears a collar because it will leave an unsightly impression in his hair, or worse, it will chafe the hair off under the neck. A show Doberman wears a collar only when necessary, not as everyday neckwear.

Show Dobermans sport extremely short nails. This helps show off the conformation of the foot and prevents the nails from making the toes splay. You can't achieve this type of pedicure overnight; the nail must be shortened gradually to prevent exposing the quick (the nail's nerve and blood supply). A rotary file is often used to perform this job, and you may wish to obtain expert instruction until you are confident enough to do it by yourself.

Then, of course, a Doberman needs to be groomed to perfection before strutting his stuff in the show ring. You will have to familiarize yourself with the best grooming products to use and learn tricks of the trade to show him to his best advantage. Consult with your breeder, find a mentor, or ask other exhibitors which shampoos, cream rinses, stain removers, or hot spot treatments they prefer to use. It will save you the time and expense of experimenting with all these products yourself.

Nervous About Nail Trimming?

If you are nervous about trimming your dog's nails, you have a lot of company. Many people do not feel comfortable performing this procedure. But this is no reason to allow your dog's nails to grow too long. Long nails can cause foot problems and lameness, which in turn can cause leg problems, which can then affect your dog's posture, and so on. As you can see, a nail problem works its way up the dog's body to affect his whole structure.

So, if you can't bring yourself to keep up with your dog's nail trimming, consult a professional. Veterinarians and professional groomers are willing to trim your dog's nails for a very reasonable fee.

Nail care keeps your dog's feet healthy.

NAIL CARE

Regardless of whether or not you show your dog, regular grooming of his nails, ears, eyes, and teeth can help maintain his overall health.

Nail trimming can be done at home, or by your groomer or vet if you are uncomfortable doing it yourself. If you're nervous about trimming your dog's nails for the first time, you're not alone. Understandably, almost everyone is a little apprehensive because trimming a dog's nail too short can result in cutting into the quick. When this happens, your will dog yelp and his nail will bleed profusely. To complicate matters, Dobermans have dark nails that make it extremely difficult to locate the quick visually. But there are some tricks to prevent cutting the nail too short.

Whether you use a guillotine nail clipper (one with a hole through which to place the nail and a blade that cuts across the hole) or a scissors-type nail clipper, choose a medium-sized clipper for your Doberman. Cut a small amount of nail at a time until you see a small black dot in the center of the cut surface. This is the very tip of the quick, and it is a good indication to stop trimming. You can also view the nail from the side to determine the excess growth of the nail. Because the top of the nail grows faster than the underside, excess growth creates a hook. You can clearly see where

Whether your Doberman's ears are cropped or uncropped, groom them weekly to keep them healthy.

this hook begins on the underside of the nail. If you only cut the excess growth (a little at a time if you are unsure), you will avoid cutting into the quick. Again, watch for the black dot in the center of the cut nail to help you become familiar with how much of the hook can be removed.

Overgrown nails complicate trimming because the quick lengthens as a nail grows. This is why it is best to trim nails regularly. Dogs with very long nails need to have them trimmed a little at a time over a period of weeks to get the quick to recede before the nails can be trimmed as short as they should be.

If you accidentally cut a nail too short, hold the end of a cotton swab to the tip to slow the bleeding and help the blood clot. Styptic powder also works well to stop the bleeding.

Many dogs are not fond of having their feet handled, which is another good reason to trim nails frequently. With patient and frequent handling, your dog will soon learn to accept this necessary part of grooming. Your Doberman may need his nails trimmed every two to four weeks to keep them at a proper length.

EAR CARE

There is some debate about whether uncropped ears are more prone to ear infections than cropped ears. But regardless of the type of ears your Doberman has, it is still important to inspect and clean them regularly. Wiping the ears with a cotton ball lightly saturated with rubbing alcohol once every week or two is a good preventive. The alcohol not only cleans the ears but also helps dry them out. Moisture is a key factor in allowing bacteria to multiply and cause an infection.

Mild signs of an ear infection are an odor from the ears, head shaking, or ear scratching. If the problem doesn't clear up with daily cotton and alcohol cleanings within 7 to 10 days, you should consult your veterinarian. More severe cases of ear infection can result in a very strong ear odor, red or cracked skin on the underside of the ear, and inflammation. Your dog may carry his head in a tilted position or even show some signs of dizziness or lack of balance. For these serious cases, veterinary attention should be sought immediately. Antibiotics, ear flushing, or other treatments may be necessary to get the problem under control.

EYE CARE

Sight is one of the most important senses for both dogs and humans. But unlike blind humans, who can make use of canes, seeing-eye dogs, and other devices to maintain a good quality of life, dogs aren't so fortunate. That's why it is so critical to make a habit of examining your dog's eyes during grooming.

Any sign of squinting, redness, inflammation, cloudiness, or obstruction of the lens is an indication that veterinary assistance should be sought immediately. Some eye conditions, like glaucoma, can progress very rapidly, so any problem with the eyes should be treated as an emergency.

Application of a canine eye wash can be helpful to clean and soothe your dog's eyes if they appear mildly irritated (teary) due to dust or debris. Any foreign objects that cannot be easily removed from your dog's eyes should be tended to by your vet.

DENTAL CARE

According to the American Veterinary Dental Society, 80 percent of dogs show some signs of dental disease by the age of three years. It's no wonder dental care for dogs has become such a vital part of maintenance care. With dogs living longer than ever, it's important to invest the effort necessary to keep your Doberman's teeth healthy and in his mouth as long as possible.

Wild species of canine enjoy the benefits of natural teeth

Signs of Dental Disease

- discharge from the gums
- gums that bleed easily
- halitosis (bad breath)
- loose teeth
- loss of weight
- mouth pain or refusal to eat
- pawing at the mouth
- receding gum line
- red or swollen gums
- yellow or discolored teeth

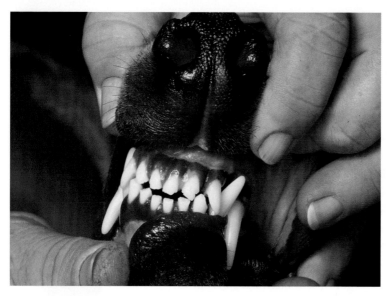

Inspect and clean your dog's teeth as part of his regular grooming routine.

cleaning from the foods they eat. The fibrous tissues and bones of prey help scrape and remove any food residue that accumulates. Domesticated dogs, on the other hand, consume foods that stick to the teeth and develop into plaque and tartar. Moist or wet foods are notorious for leaving residue, and dry foods crack and crumble before they can scrape and clean the portion of the teeth along the gum line. The accumulation of plaque and tartar eventually works its way under the gums, where bacteria begin to thrive and multiply. The bacteria may cause infections in the mouth that can subsequently travel throughout the circulatory system to infect other parts of the body. A dog with serious periodontal disease can become very sick indeed.

Choosing Dental Care Products

Because we have taken dogs out of their wild environment and subjected them to commercial foods that cause this problem, we need take steps to compensate for the dental care otherwise provided by Mother Nature. Many products are on the market to help with this job, including dental chews and bones like the ones made by Nylabone. But while dental chews and bones help remove food particles from the teeth, brushing helps to further remove plaque buildup along the gum line.

Tooth brushing kits come with either finger applicators or brushes, and you can choose whichever is most comfortable for your dog and is easiest for you to use. Doggy toothpastes are specially formulated and have a pleasant taste that will ensure your dog's cooperation.

How to Brush Your Dog's Teeth

When you are ready to incorporate dental care into your

Banishing Bad Breath

When your guests shirk away from your Doberman's friendly kisses, it is a good indication that your canine companion suffers from the most despicable of doggy odors—dog breath. Some cases of bad breath are caused by bacteria in the mouth and are a sign of poor dental care. To minimize odor, keep your dog's teeth brushed, or schedule a professional cleaning with your veterinarian if his dental condition requires it.

Even with the best dental care, some dogs can still melt steel with a pant of their breath. Bad breath isn't always a sign of dental disease, however, but rather of what your dog eats. Horses have pleasantly sweet breath because they eat fresh grass and fragrant alfalfa. Dogs have "dog breath" because they eat meat. Teeth brushing may not always address this problem because canine toothpastes are designed to taste good to dogs, not necessarily to smell good to humans. But all is not lost. You can still combat dog breath with some of the new, innovative dental products now on the market, such as the ones made by Nylabone. Breath strips or wipes can help sweeten your dog's breath; dental wipes that contain baking soda are especially effective. With regular care, perhaps the day will come when "dog breath" will no longer be a derogatory term!

grooming routine, introduce your dog to this process gradually. First, let him taste some of the toothpaste to spark his interest, and then brush only his front teeth. Each time you brush, work a few more teeth into your dental regimen until you can eventually brush all his teeth without protest. Most dogs, both young and old, will adjust quite well to this routine, and you will soon be able to check and clean your dog's teeth with little time or effort.

Brushing once or twice a week is the best way to prevent dental problems, but brushing is just a preventive and not a cure. If your dog already exhibits signs of dental disease, consult your veterinarian. He may recommend a professional teeth cleaning in which he will remove the accumulation of plaque and tartar while your dog is under anesthesia. Regular brushing afterward will help keep your dog's teeth in good condition.

If you look at grooming as an opportunity to enjoy and spend time with your dog, all the other benefits that come from it are icing on the cake. Your dog will look and feel good, and this will reflect in his attitude. You, too, will find it hard not to be proud of his appearance. In addition to being twice as huggable, a clean dog will leave less hair and dander in your home. Best yet, regular grooming helps keep your Doberman healthy, something worth more than money. So enjoy grooming time, bask in the results, and go out and show off your dog!

TRAINING *and* BEHAVIOR
of Your Doberman Pinscher

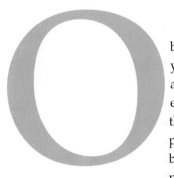

Observing a well-trained dog can almost bring tears to your eyes. It's impossible not to admire a dog whose attention is intensely focused on his master and who executes commands as if he were oblivious to the rest of the world. How does someone train a dog to become so precisely obedient and responsive? Does the dog have to be exceptionally intelligent, or does his owner have to be a particularly talented trainer? No. Anyone (even you!) can train a dog to almost any degree of obedience. The secret is learning how to go about it and putting the necessary time into it.

But there's more at stake than creating a canine companion you can enjoy and your acquaintances can admire. Some dogs make relatively good pets with hardly any training at all, but the Doberman is not one of them. Independent-minded, physically powerful, and naturally protective, a Doberman who cannot be controlled can become a horrendous nuisance. So if you do not have the time or ambition to train your Doberman, you would be better off with another breed.

Training is the greatest investment you can make in your Doberman's future. Learning how to communicate with your dog, using effective training techniques, and knowing how to solve problem behaviors or where to seek help, are the keys to successful training.

TRAINING BASICS

Training relies on communicating with a dog. Communication isn't a matter of telling your dog what to do and expecting him to obey, it is a two-way discourse where you and your dog listen and talk to each other. To teach your dog how to understand your language, you have to learn to understand some of his.

Learning Your Dog's Language

Unlike humans, dogs are not capable of a great variety of vocal sounds, so they rely quite heavily on body language. They are experts at interpreting visual cues, which is why they respond so well to hand signals. Understanding what your dog is saying through

Dogs love to please their owners, and they learn quickly and effectively when training is a positive experience.

his body movements and vocalizations, as well as how your own body language affects him, can be very helpful during the training process.

Training Methods

There are many different ways to teach a dog any given skill, but some methods are obviously better than others. Overly harsh methods can make dogs fearful and hamper learning, they can traumatize sensitive or shy dogs, and they can make aggressive dogs more aggressive. Positive training methods, on the other hand, foster interest in and enthusiasm for learning. They build confidence and trust in your dog rather than fear, and they make training much more enjoyable for both of you. Training should be a fun activity, not military boot camp!

Positive training focuses on enlisting your dog's cooperation instead of forcing him to do something. Wouldn't you rather have your Doberman respond to you willingly, with a sparkle in his eye and a wag of his stubby tail, rather than reluctantly out of coercion? The days of hitting, jerking leashes, and physically forcing a dog to submit are gone. Your dog is not a robot. He is a thinking, breathing creature who feels both joy and pain. If you love your dog, you will train him with joy, not pain.

Getting your dog to do what you want involves teaching him how to do something and then conditioning him to do it each time you give him a command. Four principles of shaping canine behavior will determine how effectively you communicate with him: positive reinforcement, repetition, negative reinforcement, and consistency.

Positive Reinforcement

Shaping canine behavior in a positive way begins with offering rewards as positive reinforcement for desired behaviors. Rewards can consist of treats, praise, petting, or playing with a favorite toy. They convince your dog that doing the desired behavior is obviously in his best interest. But in order for rewards to be effective, they must be offered *immediately* when a desired behavior is performed so your dog can associate the reward with that specific behavior.

In an effort to make this association as obvious as possible, many trainers now use handheld clickers to let the dog know instantly that he has performed correctly. A dog quickly learns that when he hears a click, he will be rewarded. Another method that doesn't require a free hand to manipulate a clicker is to say "Yes!," followed by a reward, each time your dog executes a correct behavior.

Repetition

Rewards make it easy for a dog to understand what it is you want him to do, and they can also encourage him to repeat a desired behavior. Repetition is what conditions a dog to respond automatically (without having to think about it) to a command. It is also a form of practice to keep his skills honed.

You probably don't remember some of the things you learned in school because you don't use that information in your daily life. Dogs, too, suffer from forgetfulness if training is not practiced on a regular basis. Mental exercises are subject to the "if you don't use

Training Tips

The following basic training principles will help you and your Doberman achieve your training goals:

- learn patience
- teach hand signals
- establish eye contact and name recognition
- keep training sessions short

Desired behaviors should always be rewarded. Even after food rewards have been withdrawn, praise and petting are in order whenever your dog behaves appropriately. This consistent reinforcement will ensure his continuing cooperation, fuel his desire to please you, and keep your lines of communication open.

it, you lose it" rule. So even after your dog has become well trained, put him through his paces now and then to keep him conditioned and responsive.

Negative Reinforcement

People don't like to use the word "punishment" these days because it is associated with physical retribution, which isn't necessarily true. Punishment, or negative reinforcement, can be just as important as positive reinforcement in shaping canine behavior. Positive reinforcement encourages desired behavior, while negative reinforcement discourages undesired behavior. The combination of these elements help to make it easy for your dog to do the right thing and difficult for him to do the wrong thing.

Punishment does not need to be harsh or cruel. The purpose of negative reinforcement is not to harm your dog physically or emotionally. Positive dog trainers prefer to use negative punishment, which involves taking something away from your dog that he wants. For instance, if your dog jumps on you, turn away from him and take away your attention, which is the thing he wanted when he jumped on you in the first place. If your dog pulls on the leash, turn and walk in another direction to deny him what he most desires: to keep going forward. (In contrast, *positive punishment* involves giving your dog something that he doesn't want, which includes jerking his leash, shaking him by the scruff, or other aversive reprimands. Many trainers and owners consider these methods to be inhumane.)

Negative reinforcement works much the same way as positive reinforcement in that it has to be imposed *immediately* after an inappropriate behavior so that your dog can associate the consequence with his behavior. But negative reinforcement alone is not always enough to discourage undesirable behavior. You may also need to replace your dog's inappropriate behavior with an appropriate behavior. In this way, you will set your dog up to succeed so that you can reward him. When your dog jumps on you, take away your attention but then ask him to sit. When he sits, reward him. When your dog pulls on the leash and you change directions to discourage him, tell him to heel as he comes back up to your side, and then reward him. This way, instead of just telling your dog what *not* to do, you are teaching your dog what *to* do.

Negative reinforcement can be very effective in discouraging natural or instinctual canine behaviors that humans find annoying—like jumping, digging, or pulling on the leash—but they should not be used in the process of teaching your dog new skills. For example, if you're teaching your dog to lie down and he rolls onto his back instead, simply ignore the incorrect response and try again. If you punish your dog because he "got an answer wrong" during training, you will severely dampen his desire to learn. It is also not fair to use negative reinforcement as a replacement for proper management and supervision. Dogs who are left unattended for long periods of time will often engage in undesirable behaviors out of boredom or loneliness, and these problems should be addressed with management methods such as confinement, supervision, or activities, rather than punishment.

Consistency

Consistency in training methods, in your use of rewards, and in consequences make it clear to your dog exactly what you expect of him. This is the single most important element of training! No matter how good the training method, how scrumptious the reward, or how convincing the consequence, you will not be able to effectively train your dog without consistency.

Consistency greatly enhances communication with your dog and gives him a sense of security. Knowing what is expected of him, and what he can expect from you, builds the trust and respect that are so important in the training process. Always ask your dog to perform a particular behavior using the same cue word such as "*sit*," rather than replacing it occasionally with "*sit down*" or "*I said, sit!*" When correcting inappropriate behaviors like digging, chewing, or begging, be consistent in never allowing these behaviors to occur.

Getting Your Dog's Attention

Now that you know the basic elements necessary for effectively shaping your dog's behavior, you are ready to begin communicating with him, building a rapport, and embarking on your journey to create the perfect canine companion. But there is one thing you need to know about communication in general: You can't communicate with your dog (or a person, for that matter) if you don't have his attention.

Your dog needs to look at you if he is to receive your messages

Look at Me, I'm Talking to You

Some trainers prefer to use a specific command like Look! or Look at me! to instruct a dog to pay attention. This command can be taught the same way as teaching your dog to respond to his name: by rewarding him each time he looks at you whenever you give him the command.

clearly. If he is concerned about what the other dogs in training class are doing, if he's focused on the kids playing in the other room, or if he's preoccupied with anything else in the environment, he is not receptive to your communication.

If your dog responds well to his name, gain his attention simply by saying his name before asking him to do something. Heighten his responsiveness by carrying treats in your pocket during the day, saying his name occasionally, and then rewarding him each time he looks at you.

Length, Frequency, and Location of Training

Even a very attentive dog will begin to lose concentration during training if the lesson is too long. Puppies and young dogs, in particular, have limited attention spans. Keep your dog sharp during training by limiting training sessions to 5 to 10 minutes for puppies and young dogs, and 15 to 20 minutes for adult dogs. Vary the skills you are working on during training to keep your dog's interest level high.

There is no maximum limit on the frequency of training sessions, as long as they re not scheduled too close together. If you really enjoy training, you may opt to train as often as twice per day, although care must be taken to avoid giving your dog too many food rewards! For the well-trained Doberman of your dreams, a minimum of three training sessions per week will allow your dog to progress at a reasonable rate.

Initially, your training sessions must be conducted in a quiet location so that your dog can concentrate on the tasks at hand. When your dog responds perfectly in this type of environment, you will need to proof him by reviewing what he has learned in more distracting locations. This will teach him to respond consistently anywhere you take him. Training classes, dog parks, or places where other dogs are present provide tempting distractions.

After your dog is proficient in basic obedience in a variety of situations, reduce training sessions to once per week to keep his skills in top form. Use this opportunity to teach him something new once in awhile. By challenging your dog to learn new things, you are keeping him mentally active. Dobermans thrive on having the opportunity to use their intellectual abilities, and you'll be amazed at what your canine Einstein can learn to do!

For best results, keep training sessions short and vary the skills you are working on to keep your dog's interest level high.

TRAINING A PUPPY

Training your Doberman puppy begins the moment you bring him home. Whether you intend to teach him or not, he is learning. This is why it is a good idea to formulate household rules in advance, so they can be enforced from the very beginning.

Your puppy is never too young to learn, but it will take time before his young mind retains everything. Keep patience in your back pocket at all times. With a lot of repetition and consistency, your pup will eventually begin to understand what is expected of him.

Crate Training

Situations will always arise when you must crate your dog: trips to the vet's office, short absences from the home, or excursions to the dog show. Dogs who are not accustomed to a crate will whine, bark, pace, and claw at the door trying to get out. Wouldn't it be nice if your dog accepted his crate without all the fussing?

The Purpose of Crate Training

Crate training taps into your dog's natural den instinct, which is his innate preference for a small, cozy place to call his own. Wild canines find comfort and security in the dens they dig out of the earth, and your dog can find the same protective security within the confines of his crate. Crate training not only eliminates annoying crate behaviors, it also reduces stress and anxiety for your dog.

Crate training, however, is *not* a method of confining a puppy for long periods of time to prevent housetraining accidents or household damage. A long period of confinement in such a small space is physically and emotionally unhealthy for any dog. Puppies need room for exercise to help their growing bones and muscles. They also need an appropriate place to relieve themselves because they do not yet have the bladder and bowel control that adult dogs do, so they need to eliminate more often. You do not want to put your puppy in the position of having to eliminate in his crate.

The crate can be a useful tool for transporting, temporarily housing, or housetraining your dog, but it is not much good for any of these purposes if your puppy constantly messes in it. If you must confine your puppy for periods longer than a couple of hours, it is best to keep him in a puppy-proofed room or puppy pen.

Keeping It Positive

Never use a crate as a form of punishment. Your dog cannot learn to enjoy spending time in his crate if it is associated with a negative experience. Would you rather spend time in a room you consider to be a quiet retreat or a prison cell? Always view the crate as your dog's personal territory, and keep his associations with it positive. Throughout the training process, the crate should be open and available for your puppy's use whenever he desires to use it.

Choosing an Appropriate Crate

The first step in crate training is to obtain the right sized crate for your puppy. One that is too small will be uncomfortable and quickly outgrown, and one that is too large may tempt your puppy into using a portion of it as a bathroom. To avoid having to buy different sized crates as your puppy grows, purchase the size he will use as an adult and section off the excess space. Some crates are sold with dividers that allow you to adjust the interior for your current needs.

The crate should provide enough room for your dog to stand, turn around, and lie down in comfortably. It also should offer soft bedding—it won't make a very tempting den if it is not

Crating When You're Home

If you only crate your puppy when you leave the house, he may begin to associate it with you leaving, which may cause him to dislike his den. To prevent this, train your puppy to expect that he may sometimes need to be crated when you're at home.

Crate Confinement Guidelines for Puppies

8 to 12 weeks old	½ to 1 hour
12 to 16 weeks old	1 to 3 hours
16 to 20 weeks old	3 to 5 hours
20 to 24 weeks old	5 to 6 hours
24+ weeks old	6 hours maximum

comfortable. Foam pads, fleece liners, or padded beds can be purchased to fit your crate, but you can also use a blanket, towels, or other soft materials, as long as they are washable and not easily shredded and consumed by your puppy.

Introducing Your Puppy to the Crate

When you are ready to begin training, place the crate in a common area of your home with the door open so your puppy can see it, smell it, and explore it. Next, put treats or toys near the entrance. If your puppy does not show any fear of the crate, advance to putting treats or toys just inside the door so that he'll put his head inside. Gradually start putting the objects of his desire further into the crate until your puppy enters it of his own will.

Don't rush this training process because your puppy may become fearful of the crate—take your time and advance slowly. When he is comfortable entering it on his own, teach him to do this on command by putting a treat in the crate and saying, *"kennel"* or *"crate."* Eventually, you can condition him to enter the crate when you give the command, and then reward him when he complies.

The next step is to start closing the door to the crate when your puppy is inside so he can get used to being confined in it. It helps to keep him busy during this step by feeding him in the crate or providing a chew toy or treat-releasing toy. When he is done eating or playing, release him immediately before he shows signs of discomfort.

When he appears to tolerate this well, condition him to being confined for longer periods of time. Always make sure your pup has a potty break prior to confinement, and again, put toys in the crate to keep him busy and happy. Confinement may be maintained for 10 to 20 minutes at first, and then gradually increased.

Avoiding Problems With Crate Training

If your puppy begins to fuss during crate training, it is *very* important not to give in to his protests and let him out. This will only teach him that if he fusses, he will be released. Always wait until he is calm and quiet before letting him out. He will soon learn that you are in control and that fussing has no rewards.

If you leave home while your puppy is confined, keep departures and arrivals as tranquil as possible. Giving your puppy too much attention prior to leaving can heighten his anxiety about being left alone. By approaching crate training in a positive way, taking it one step at a time, and focusing on keeping your puppy comfortable, the crate can become a valuable method of confinement and a comfortable place of rest for your dog.

Housetraining

There are some canine behaviors you may be willing to tolerate or make concessions to manage, but house soiling is probably not one of them! A dog who is not housetrained just doesn't make a very good house pet. Of course, you want to housetrain your puppy as quickly as possible, but success isn't determined solely on the training methods you use. Your puppy's maturity and bladder and bowel control have a lot to do with how quickly he can be trained. So be realistic in your expectations.

Managing your puppy correctly until he is reliably housetrained can minimize accidents, cleanup, and floor damage, as well as a lot of frustration on your part. Restrict your puppy to certain areas of the house where he can be closely supervised. When you can't be there to watch him, put him in a puppy-proof room or puppy pen that offers a suitable place for him to do his business.

Using a Designated Area

Before you begin housetraining, select an outdoor spot where your puppy will be taken for potty breaks. Using the same area for this purpose has several advantages: You can choose a spot where your lawn or landscaping won't be damaged, the scents in the designated area will encourage him to keep using it, and he will learn that he is not outside to play but to do his business.

Puppies between 8 and 16 weeks old should be taken to their potty spot at least every 1 to 2 hours, but in most cases your puppy will set the schedule. He is most likely to eliminate after waking,

When housetraining your Doberman, choose a spot in your yard where you want him to eliminate and take him to that same area every time.

eating, or playing, so take him out at these times and observe him closely in between. If he suddenly stops what he's doing to sniff the floor while circling or pacing back and forth in one area, he's getting ready to lighten his load, so take him outside immediately.

Handling Accidents

Some accidents are inevitable and should be expected. If you catch your puppy eliminating in the house, scoop him up and rush him to his potty spot. You can tell him *"outside,"* but do not scold or punish him. Making him fearful during the housetraining process can make it even more difficult. Most important, never punish him after the fact because this will only confuse him and cause him stress.

Clean up any accidents promptly, and treat the area with a pet stain and odor remover. It is crucial to eliminate any remaining scent so your puppy will not be tempted to use the spot again. A number of products are available specifically formulated to break down pet urine and destroy the odor. Some household cleaners are also effective, as stated on their packages, but do not use any product containing ammonia because it will intensify the natural ammonia scent of the urine.

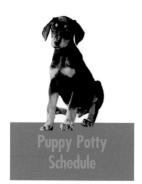

Puppy Potty Schedule

A good rule of thumb to use when determining how often your Doberman pup may need to relieve himself is to calculate one hour for each month of age. For example, a three-month-old puppy cannot wait any longer than three hours between potty breaks. Exercise and fluid consumption will obviously affect the frequency of your puppy's need to eliminate, so keep this in mind when developing a potty break schedule or when crating him.

Housetraining When You're Not Home

If you are gone for a good portion of the day, your puppy should be kept in an area that offers an appropriate place to eliminate because he cannot be expected to hold it for long periods of time. Newspapers are often the toilet material of choice, and you can encourage your puppy to use them by always saving a piece of soiled newspaper to lay down with the clean supply.

The area you designate for your puppy's safekeeping while you are gone should always be kept as clean as possible. Dogs raised in a filthy environment are much more difficult to housetrain, while those raised in a clean environment learn to prefer cleanliness. Clean his area daily or more frequently if possible. You can't expect your puppy to eventually keep your house clean if he becomes accustomed to living in his accumulated waste.

Most of the frustration associated with housetraining is caused by unrealistic expectations. It may take a few months to reliably housetrain your puppy, so be prepared for this. Supervise and observe your puppy closely, take him to his potty spot consistently, and keep his living area clean. When managed properly, housetraining can be much less stressful and more easily tolerated.

COMMON PUPPY BEHAVIORS

Puppies engage in a number of behaviors that are very natural for them but cause problems for their humans. Knowing how to handle these behaviors will help teach your puppy how to live with you more harmoniously.

Chewing

Puppies must chew on things to ease the discomfort of teething, but they also like to use their mouths for things besides chewing. Like babies, they are always exploring their environment. They like to taste and test the firmness of things with their mouths. Unfortunately, your puppy may try to teethe on or taste test the legs of your oak dining table or antique china cabinet.

You can't expect your puppy not to chew, but you can teach him to chew on appropriate items. Be sure to provide plenty of chew toys that offer various textures, hardness, sizes, and shapes, like the ones Nylabone makes. When you find your puppy targeting inappropriate items, tell him "*no!*" in a firm voice and then redirect him to a more acceptable item. Your puppy will soon learn which chew things are acceptable and which are not.

Meanwhile, it helps to limit temptations by removing certain items from his environment. If you are accustomed to leaving your shoes by the door, or your children are in the habit of leaving toys lying on the floor, now is the time to tidy up your house a bit. You can prevent a lot of damage simply by making inappropriate chew things inaccessible. For everything else, you will have to supervise your puppy closely to prevent damage.

Play Biting

Puppies also like to use their mouths in play. They learned early on from their littermates that it's perfectly acceptable to nip and bite while frolicking with each other, so it's not surprising that they like to bite at fingers and hands when playing with humans. This may seem cute at first, and perfectly tolerable, until your puppy grows a little bigger and the nips become more aggressive and painful. Therefore it's best to discourage this behavior from the start.

If your puppy tries to bite at your hands or other parts of your body, offer him a more acceptable plaything to bite. You can shake a tug rope or other toy in front of him to encourage him to take it in his mouth. If he persists in going after your hands, say *"no bite"* in a firm voice and withhold your attention from him for a while. There is no worse consequence for a puppy than to end his play time! Withholding your attention will also give him a chance to settle down if he has become too rambunctious.

If you consistently do not allow your puppy to bite you, he will eventually learn that human hands (and other body parts) are off limits. This is an important lesson that will follow him into adulthood. Dogs who have not been taught to inhibit biting are more likely to develop problems with aggressive biting later.

FORMAL OBEDIENCE CLASSES

Sure, you can train your dog at home, but there are a lot of advantages to enrolling in a formal obedience class. The expert advice, guidance, and instruction of a professional trainer are invaluable. You can learn how to understand your dog better, how to communicate with him more effectively, and find out how to

Why Do Puppies Chew?

Puppies chew because they enjoy exploring the tastes and textures of objects in their environment. They also need to relieve the discomforts of teething.

Obedience classes are especially recommended for Dobermans because it is very important for this independent-minded, protective dog to learn self-control and to be thoroughly socialized.

solve training problems that might be difficult for you to resolve on your own.

Training classes are especially recommended for Dobermans because it is very important for this independent-minded, protective dog to learn self-control and to be thoroughly socialized. The training class environment offers various distractions that can help you train your dog to be more reliable and consistent. Besides, it's always fun to get together with other dog lovers!

Choosing a Trainer

Training instructors are individuals who each have their own strengths and weaknesses. Some are better communicators, some are more knowledgeable, and some have more experience than others. The best way to separate the good trainers from the less desirable ones is to interview them by phone, or better yet, observe them at work. Most trainers will accommodate you if you wish to sit in on one of their training sessions.

These are some of the questions you should ask:

- **What kind of training methods do you use?** Seek a trainer who uses positive training methods. Any trainer who still uses methods that involve using choke collars, jerking the leash, or forcefulness should be avoided because this is an indication that she does not have current knowledge of dog behavior and training.

- **What kind of experience and credentials do you have?** Membership with a dog training organization like the Association of Pet Dog Trainers (APDT) is not a guarantee of quality, but it does indicate a trainer takes her job seriously. If she has obtained a title such as Certified Pet Dog Trainer (CPDT), she has met certain educational requirements.

- **How many students are typically in a class?** The larger the class, the less individual attention you will receive. A good trainer will limit attendance to six or seven students per class.

- **How long are the training sessions?** Forty-five minutes is a good length for training sessions. Some sessions run for an hour, but you can expect your dog to become bored, tired, and unfocused toward the end of the session. Sessions over an hour are too long.

  When observing a class, watch for the following:

- **How does the trainer communicate?** Does she explain things so everyone can understand without using a lot of technical jargon? Does she communicate just as effectively with people as she does with dogs? Does she present things in an upbeat manner?

- **How does she handle training problems?** Does she offer effective solutions? Does she have more than one solution for a problem? Are solutions tailored to fit the individual dog and owner, or does she have a one-size-fits-all approach to training problems? Does she appear to be knowledgeable about dog behavior?

- **Are the students and dogs happy to be there?** Is training a fun experience for them, or do they seem frustrated and stressed?

- **Does the trainer appear impatient, frustrated, or angry at any time during the class?** These emotions are roadblocks to learning and have no place in the training environment.

BASIC OBEDIENCE SKILLS

Regardless of your dog's purpose, whether he is intended to be a loving family companion, a working dog, or destined to achieve greatness on the agility course or in the conformation ring, basic obedience training is a must. Basic obedience includes a number of skills considered the minimum training requirements for any dog. Besides teaching your dog manners, basic obedience is the foundation of control and the stepping-stone to any other type of training.

The *Come* Command

Come is the single most important command you can teach your dog. A dog who doesn't come when called can become lost or injured, not to mention becoming a neighborhood nuisance. Unfortunately, this is also one of the most difficult skills to train your dog to perform consistently.

When your puppy is small, he follows you everywhere, he never wanders too far, and he always comes running when you call, so you think you nailed the *come* command at an early age. But your puppy has simply replaced his main source of security—his mother—with you, and stays close by instinct. When he gets a little older, he'll begin to explore. His desires will become more important than yours, and he'll begin to test your control. That's when you'll find yourself chasing your dog around the block, futilely calling his name and threatening harsh punishment.

Older dogs, as well, may not respond consistently to the *come* command. They need time to accept their new owners before they will become respectful and obedient. They need time to learn their new boundaries before they will limit their territory to your yard.

Practice Come *Frequently*

You must keep your dog leashed or fenced when outdoors until he can be taught to come reliably. This is a skill that should be taught constantly, in a variety of environments and situations, and with various distractions. Teach it in your house, teach it in the yard, and teach it while out for walks. Frequent conditioning will eventually have your dog responding automatically to this command without questioning it.

While in your home, carry treats in your pocket and call your dog occasionally from different rooms. Reward him promptly each time he comes when called. When in a fenced enclosure, wait until your dog is distracted, then call him. Reward him each time he comes. When in open areas outdoors, use a long leash or rope so your dog can explore some distance away from you, then try calling him.

The purpose of the long leash is to keep your dog safe by

Basic Commands

The following basic commands will help you establish some control over your dog's behavior:

- come (recall)
- sit
- down
- stay
- heel

preventing him from running off, not to force him to come to you if he does not obey the command. If you force him to come by pulling on the leash, he will quickly learn that compliance is only necessary when he is on a leash. The moment he gets loose, obedience will be optional!

Keep **Come** *Positive*

When disciplining your dog during training the *come* command, a very important rule to remember is to never punish him when he comes to you, even if he was initially disobedient. It is natural to want to discipline him for his bad behavior, but if you punish him when he comes to you, he will not be so inclined to come to you the next time. In fact, he will be more likely to avoid you. If you even call him in an angry voice, you will be encouraging him to stay away from you rather than to come, so keep your voice happy and upbeat.

Come is the single most important command you can teach your dog. A dog who doesn't come when called can become lost or injured.

When Your Dog Won't Obey **Come**

Running off and ignoring your commands to *come* can become an annoying habit on the part of your dog and a serious problem for you. You can prevent getting into this situation in the first place by being vigilant about never letting your Doberman loose until he is reliably trained to come when called. Still, the chance always exists that he will manage to get loose anyway. He may get out the door when company arrives, or he may jump out of the car before you manage to get a leash on him.

If this happens, call your dog in a happy voice and slap your thighs in an invitation to play. Another incentive for your dog to come to you is to call him and run in the opposite direction—dogs love to play chase! If these techniques don't work, try coaxing your dog to come by saying a key word to which he will respond, such as "treat," or "cookie." Or, you can say "Let's go!" and open a car door, or "Let's go for a walk!" Few dogs can resist the opportunity for a car ride or a walk. Be prepared to deliver on these promises if your dog comes to you.

If you consistently reward your dog each and every time he comes, he will learn that obeying the *come* command doesn't mean the fun will end. Take your dog for a walk or play a little game of fetch. He will soon realize that it is in his best interest to obey when you call him.

When Dogs Like to Explore

Running off tends to be a greater problem for young or recently acquired dogs. Most of us can tell when someone in the neighborhood has gotten a new dog or when a young dog has reached the exploratory age—often called a dog's teenage years at 6 to 18 months—because the dog usually makes his rounds of the neighborhood sooner or later. Teaching your new dog not to rush out the door can help prevent this problem, and consistently training the *come* command will eventually resolve it.

Most young dogs who run just want to explore. If you let your dog explore a little bit to let him burn off some excess energy and satisfy some of his adventurous spirit before attempting to call him, he will be more willing to come. Follow him for a while to keep tabs on his location and walk parallel to him so you do not chase him farther away. Once caught, you should *always* reward your dog because you really didn't catch him at all. There isn't a human on the face of the earth who can run as fast as a healthy Doberman, so if you managed to get your hands on your dog, it's because he let you.

The *Sit* Command

Reliability isn't as difficult to attain with the *sit* command because it is one of the easiest skills for a dog to learn. Dogs who appear to have very little training at all seem to know this command if they know nothing else. This is because sitting is a very natural and comfortable position for a dog—which is a good thing, too, because the *sit* is a very useful command to use to get your dog under control. It is also the starting position for a number of other skills, such as *down* and *stay*.

Sometimes, all you need to do is hold a treat above your dog's head, just behind his eyes—not so high that it causes him to jump up for it, but high enough to make him look up. When your dog's

Getting Your Dog's Attention

It's impossible not to admire a dog whose attention is intensely focused on his master and who executes commands as if he were oblivious to the rest of the world. Learning how to communicate with your dog and using effective training techniques are the keys to successful training. But you can't communicate with him if you don't have his attention. Your dog needs to look at you if he is to receive your messages clearly. If your Doberman responds well to his name, gain his attention simply by saying his name before asking him to do something. Heighten his responsiveness by carrying treats in your pocket during the day, saying his name occasionally, and then rewarding him each time he looks at you.

head rises, it is natural for his back end to drop, and he may just plop into a sit without much effort at all. Don't forget to say "Yes!" and reward your dog immediately. If this doesn't accomplish the task, you can train the *sit* command with your dog on a leash and gently pull the leash upward and backward to get your dog to rise in the front and back up slightly into a sit. You can offer further physical assistance by scooping his rear legs under his rump with one hand while operating the leash with the other. A few repetitions with prompt rewards will have your dog sitting like a pro.

The *Down* Command

The *down* command is slightly more difficult to teach than the *sit*. Even though dogs tend to lie down a lot, they only feel comfortable doing it when they're tired. Asking a dog to lie down when he is full of energy and excited about receiving training treats can be a little challenging. But *down* is a very important position to teach because it can be used to get an excited dog to settle down or to instruct your dog how to behave when people are dining.

It is easiest to teach this command when your dog is sitting because half his body will already be in a *down* position. Hold a treat on the ground in front of him so that he drops his head, and then slowly draw the treat farther away from him. The goal is to get your dog to stretch his body out in pursuit of the treat so that he will eventually drop the front end of his body into a *down*. If your dog lowers his front end even slightly, let him know immediately that he is progressing in the right direction by saying "Yes!" and giving him his reward. Rewarding partial success will keep him from becoming frustrated and will encourage him to keep trying. With each successive attempt, ask your dog to lower his front end a little more before rewarding him. It may take a few training sessions to get him to respond to the *down* command consistently.

The *Stay* Command

Stay is a relatively easy command to teach as long as the training process is done gradually. This command can greatly improve your dog's safety; you will be able to keep him from rushing out the door, running into the road, or getting into other dangerous situations if you can teach him to maintain his place.

This command must be taught in three phases: Your dog must learn to keep his position at different distances from you, for varying periods of time, and also when you are out of sight. Work on distance first by placing your dog in a sitting or standing position in front of you and telling him to *stay* (you can use the hand signal of extending your arm with your flat palm facing your dog if you desire). If he doesn't change position, indicate his correct response by saying, "Yes!" and rewarding him. Then tell your dog to *stay* and take one step backward away from him. If he still doesn't move, step toward him immediately and reward him.

Progressively increase the distance between you and your dog, each time returning immediately to reward him for the proper

Basic obedience commands like the sit-stay *are the foundation for good manners and all future learning.*

response. If, at any time, he breaks his position and tries to come to you, back up a few steps in your training and decrease the distance. Once your dog stays consistently at a good distance, begin to lengthen the amount of time you require him to stay. Again, approach this training gradually by waiting only a few seconds before returning to your dog to reward him and working up to longer lengths of time before doing so.

Once your dog understands that he must stay regardless of the distance or length of time, you can begin to train him to stay even when you are out of sight. While your dog is maintaining a *stay*, step out of the room for a brief second and immediately return to reward him if he does not break position. If he does break position, do not reward him. Instead, take him back to the original spot in which you asked him to stay and try again. When he realizes he must stay even when you leave the room, gradually increase the time you require him to stay while you are out of sight.

Walking on a Loose Leash and Heeling

Walking your dog should be a pleasure—not just for your dog, but for you, too! But it isn't much fun when your powerful Doberman dislocates your shoulder while taking what should be a leisurely stroll around the neighborhood. Teaching your dog to walk on a loose leash is definitely a course in good manners, but you might be interested in teaching your dog the more precise command to *heel* if you have aspirations of moving on to advanced obedience skills.

Dogs love to run and romp when outdoors, so it's not surprising they tend to resist the slower rate of travel of their human partners by pulling on the leash. The best way to convince a dog to walk at your slower pace is to show him that he will travel even more slowly if he pulls. When your dog pulls, abruptly stop and say "Walk nice." He may turn to look at you, wondering what's going on, or begin to walk around impatiently. In either case, if he releases tension on the leash, you can proceed walking again. It may take a number of repetitions, but eventually your dog will learn that he won't be going anywhere at all if he keeps pulling.

If your dog has exceptional difficulty learning this lesson, or if you want to teach him the *heel* command, abruptly turn around and walk in the opposite direction when he pulls. When your dog comes up to your side to catch up with you, reward him with a

Training for a Perfect Pet

Training can make the difference between owning a dog who is a cherished pet and owning one who is a terror on four legs. According to a survey conducted by the National Council on Pet Population Study and Policy (NCPPSP), over 90 percent of the dogs relinquished to animal shelters never received any formal obedience training.

food treat. Encourage him to stay by your left side by holding treats in your left hand near your left leg, and reward him frequently as long as he maintains his position there. If you do this while issuing the command to *heel*, he will soon learn to stay at your side on command.

HOUSEHOLD MANNERS

Every home and living situation is unique. Your particular situation may require you to set specific limits for your dog in your home. You may not want him on the furniture or in restricted areas. These rules should be established and enforced from the first moment your dog or puppy enters your home.

Off-Limits Furniture

Whether or not you allow your dog on your furniture is a personal decision. Dobermans, being large dogs, tend to take up a lot of room on the couch or bed. You may have newer furniture you want to preserve, or your furniture may be the type that tends to trap dog hair in the fabric or becomes easily punctured by long, tough nails. Dobermans do, however, have the kind of short, clean coat that makes them more acceptable as couch partners than other dogs, so it's not out of the question if you want to share your soft leisurely places with your dog.

In any case, there may be at least some furniture you want to keep off limits to your dog. You can teach your dog which items are not acceptable for his use by giving him an *off* command and encouraging him to vacate willingly for a food reward or doggy toy. It is important to then direct him to a more appropriate place to lie down, preferably a dog bed stationed in the same room. Your dog will soon learn where he is or is not welcome to relax.

Keeping Your Dog Off Furniture When You're Not Home

One thing to note about keeping your dog off the furniture is that your training may have little effect when you are not there to enforce the rules. Soft couches, recliners, and beds are an irresistible temptation for canines, and you cannot expect your dog to have the same self-control as humans when left unsupervised. You wouldn't be the first to discover dog hair on the furniture after an absence. In fact, some dogs have perfectly wonderful manners when their owners are home but become quite cunning in sneaking a nap on the couch when their people aren't home.

You must take proactive measures to keep your dog off the furniture when you are gone. Restrict him from spaces that have furniture you don't want him to touch by closing doors, putting up door gates, or confining him to a particular room or dog crate. Various products on the market will discourage your dog from using the furniture in your absence, such as electronic mats. Or, use other deterrents, like placing tape on the furniture with the sticky side up or plastic carpet runners laid with the pointy side up.

The only problem with these types of deterrents is that they must be placed on the furniture every time you leave the house. Your Doberman is bright enough to realize when you have forgotten to protect your furniture! They are also unsightly additions to your décor when unexpected company shows up. You may just decide the best course of action is to give in to this common canine behavior and protect your furniture by covering it with an attractive blanket or throw that can be easily washed.

Rushing Out the Door

Some dogs delight in rushing out the door as soon as it is opened, creating a hazard for people who may be entering or

Say Yes Instead of No

When a new puppy or dog joins a household, there is much he needs to learn. Until he has learned household rules and proper manners, his owner may be challenged with a variety of troublesome behaviors. It is very easy to fall into the habit of screaming, "No!" when he gets into trouble, but this word can become overused and misused, resulting in a lack of effectiveness.

Positive guidance can help you change the focus from telling your dog what *not* to do, to telling your dog what *to* do. Replacing the word "no" with consistent commands produces much better results. For example:

- When your dog jumps on forbidden furniture, direct him to get *off.*
- When your dog takes food off the coffee table, issue the command *leave it* or *don't touch.*
- If your dog enters a forbidden area, command him to *out.*
- When your dog has a desire to chase something or cross boundaries, remind him to *stay,* or call him to *come.*
- If your dog enjoys stealing your personal property, tell him to *drop it, leave it,* or *come* so that you can retrieve the item.
- During housetraining, tell your dog *outside* if you catch him having an accident, and take him outside immediately, even if he has already finished eliminating.

leaving, and also presenting a hazard for your dog if he is not yet reliably trained to come when called. This bad habit can be corrected by teaching him not to go through doors unless you instruct him to do so.

With your dog on a leash, take him to your main entry door, instruct him to *wait*, and open it just a crack. If he begins to bolt for the door, close it quickly. It helps to keep your leg poised to block him from pushing it open. Do these steps as many times as it takes for your dog to understand that you do not intend to let him out the door.

When your dog complies by not attempting to rush out the door, reward him immediately. Then begin to open the door a little more, with your leg ready to block him if he is tempted to get out. Eventually, you will be able to open it all the way. At this point, you can finally give your dog an *ok* to release him from waiting and allow him to go out. Practice will make it clear to him that he is not allowed to go through the door unless you tell him *ok*.

This skill is best practiced in a variety of locations so that your dog can learn this rule applies to all doors. Practice with all the exterior doors to your home, doors at the vet's office, doors at the pet shop, or anywhere else you take him. People will be amazed at your dog's impressive manners!

Outdoor Safety

Until your Doberman is fully boundary trained, keep him fenced or leashed for his safety whenever he spends time outdoors. Also, never leave your dog alone in your yard when you're not home.

Other Off-Limits Areas

There may be certain areas in your home that need to be off limits to your dog, such as a room filled with fine furniture and breakables, an area where other pets are fed, or a work room laden with materials that could be hazardous to him. You can teach your dog to stay out of these areas by teaching him the *out* command.

If your dog enters a forbidden area, usher him out quickly and tell him "*out*" firmly. When he is outside the area, reward him with praise or treats. With consistency, he will learn quite quickly where he is and isn't allowed to go.

Further reinforce this training by walking into the off-limits area to see if your dog follows you. If he does, escort him out with a firm *out* command and praise him whenever he respects his boundary. You can also test him by walking into the off-limits area carrying one of his toys to see if he will breach his boundary. Proper behavior in this situation deserves a lavish reward.

Reinforcing Off-Limits Areas When You're Not Home

It is not reasonable to expect your dog to respect off-limits areas when you are not present, especially if it is an area where pet food or other temptations are present. So prevent your dog's access to these areas by closing doors, putting up door gates, or restricting his boundaries while you are gone.

The *out* command can be useful for teaching your dog which outdoor areas are also off limits. Use it to designate your garden, neighbors' yards, or hazardous outdoor areas as forbidden areas, but be sure to conduct this training on a leash if your dog is not trained to recall reliably.

PROBLEM BEHAVIORS

Problem behaviors should really be called *natural* behaviors because they are behaviors dogs engage in instinctively. When your dog digs a hole in your garden, jumps on people who arrive for dinner, or shreds up a rug because he sorely misses your companionship when you are gone, you need to realize that none of these things are done with evil intent. Your dog is just being a dog! Accepting the fact that your dog is not a human will help you replace your frustration with understanding and patience.

However, just because problem behaviors are borne out of natural instinct does not mean you have to tolerate them. Your dog can be taught and conditioned to behave in ways that make him an acceptable member of your household.

Supervise your dog closely when outdoors and try to distract him with a more appropriate activity if he begins to dig.

Digging

As far as some dogs are concerned, dirt is for digging. Dogs dig to root out prey, to alleviate boredom or anxiety, to create a cool place to lie down in the summer, to escape confinement, or sometimes just for fun. They are oblivious to the fact that humans loathe holes and bare spots in their manicured lawns!

Preventing Digging

You can prevent your dog from developing this problem by not leaving him unattended outdoors for long periods of time. Boredom and loneliness will put him at high risk to start digging. Make sure you provide plenty of appropriate activities for your dog to do while outside so he doesn't discover digging as a form of amusement. Designate some toys as outdoor playthings and keep them where your dog can easily access them.

Correcting Digging

If your Doberman has already discovered the alluring pastime of exposing fresh dirt in your lawn or flower garden, supervise him closely when outdoors and try to distract him with a more appropriate activity if he begins to dig. Dobermans need an outlet for their energy, and they may find digging to be an extremely pleasurable release if their liveliness is not channeled through more appropriate activities. If your dog receives plenty of exercise and attention while outdoors, he is less likely to dig for lack of something better to do.

Sometimes, providing an appropriate place for your dog to dig can help you avoid compromising the integrity of your yard. A reasonable solution is to provide a doggy sandbox (or dirt box) in a shady area where digging is allowed. This makes a fine place to redirect your dog if he attempts to dig elsewhere, and you can encourage him to use this spot by burying treats or toys in the sand for him to dig up.

Even though you may not appreciate your dog's fine burrowing skills, it does not help to punish him for it. Punishment may serve to make the problem worse for dogs who dig to relieve anxiety. Focus on interrupting the behavior with a stern *"No!"* and directing your dog's attention elsewhere.

Jumping Up

Dogs like to greet people at face level and will often jump up to accomplish this. This behavior is quite common during puppyhood, but it becomes a monumental problem as a Doberman matures to a 75-pound (34-kg) tackler. Grandma and Grandpa certainly won't appreciate this kind of greeting when they come to visit, and neither will young children who can become seriously injured.

This is why it is best to discourage this behavior from the very beginning.

Correcting Jumping

Young dogs are exceptionally energetic and exuberant in their greetings, but you can get this vigor under control by requiring your dog to *sit* before you or any other arrivals are allowed to give him any attention. Reward your dog with petting whenever he sits nicely for greetings, but if he is exceptionally excitable, petting may be more stimulation than he can reasonably handle. In this case, avoid touching him and instruct visitors to completely ignore him until he calms down. You may also have to put your dog on a leash when people come to call so you can prevent him from jumping up until he has learned better self-control.

If your dog tries to jump on you, turn away from him and refuse to give him any attention. When he gives up and stops jumping, face him again and ask him to *sit* before rewarding him with praise, petting, or treats for good behavior. It takes a lot of persistence and consistency to convince a dog not to jump up, but you and your guests will appreciate this valuable training.

Barking

Your Doberman has been bred to be a watchdog, and as such, he has a natural instinct to alert you to what is happening in your surroundings. It would behoove you not to react to it, though, because barking is a Doberman's most noticeable method of communication. Nevertheless, always be conscious of what your dog may be trying to tell you. In some cases, excessive barking may indicate he needs more exercise and attention than you have been offering him.

As valuable as your dog's bark is to both you and him, it can be a problem when he doesn't seem to know when to stop. Incessant barking can be annoying to you, your household members, and your neighbors. At worst, it can result in nuisance complaints.

Correcting Excessive Barking

How you address this problem depends on your dog's reason for nonstop barking. If your Doberman tends to bark as an alert but then doesn't want to cease, it may be because he doesn't trust you to handle situations he considers potentially threatening. You must

Boredom and Barking

Dogs kept outdoors or in kennels can easily become chronic barkers due to boredom and lack of attention. Any slight movement or noise is likely to set them off, and their cacophony can quickly become a nuisance for the entire neighborhood. The best solution to this problem is to bring your dog indoors. Dobermans are not suited to outdoor living anyway, and they are more likely to receive adequate attention if they are kept indoors.

make it clear to him that you are his leader and you are perfectly capable of taking care of any disturbance. This is best accomplished through obedience training that establishes your leadership.

Once your leadership is no longer in question, begin to teach your dog the *quiet* command. Allow him to give proper warning, then firmly instruct him to *quiet* and distract him from the source of stimulation. If he stops barking, reward him with petting, praise, or treats. Keep in mind that it is not reasonable to expect your dog to stop barking if a stimulus is growing stronger, for instance, if a stranger is approaching your door. Wait until the person has stopped at the door before asking your dog to *quiet*.

Dogs who bark continually when confined or left alone indoors may be suffering from separation anxiety. Barking is just one of the symptoms of this problem.

Separation Anxiety

Dogs with separation anxiety may become destructive, exhibit housetraining lapses, or engage in constant barking when left alone. This problem is most prevalent in high-energy dogs like the Doberman. While humans tend to view these behaviors as spiteful, dogs really don't do things to get even with us. They do these things to vent their frustration, and punishing your dog for these behaviors will only increase his anxiety and make the problem worse.

Preventing Separation Anxiety

Preventing this problem starts with making sure your dog is comfortable when you leave the house. Feed and exercise him, give him a potty break before leaving, and make sure he is provided with soft bedding, a variety of toys to keep him busy, and fresh water. You can prevent destructive behavior and minimize housetraining lapses by confining him to a safe area and removing any temptations such as garbage receptacles, shoes, and other items from his environment.

Correcting Separation Anxiety

Dogs who become very attached to and dependent on their owners can become extremely anxious when left alone. In this case, you may have to distance yourself from your dog somewhat by avoiding excessive fondling and letting another household member

Misery Loves Company

In cases of extreme separation anxiety, people sometimes get another dog to provide company. However, if the anxiety is based on separation from you, rather than just being alone, adding a second dog may just make things worse because the dog with separation anxiety may feel that he has to fight for your attention. For some dogs, however, another dog works wonders.

Doggy day care can be another option. At these facilities, dogs get a lot of socialization and exercise, and they learn to have a good time without their owners, thus reducing their emotional dependence and lessening their separation anxiety.

To prevent separation anxiety, make sure your dog has a variety of toys to play with when he is alone.

feed him occasionally. Enrolling your dog in a doggy day care once a week may help also. If there ever were a case against developing too strong a relationship with your dog, this is it. Your dog needs to learn to be more confident and comfortable on his own.

Anxiety issues can also be reduced by keeping departures and arrivals as calm as possible. Do not fuss over your dog before you leave home, and ignore him upon your return. Do not give him any attention until he has settled down because you should only reward calm behavior. By your example, he will learn that your comings and goings are nothing to get excited about.

Some behaviorists have found success by conducting mock departures. This is when a dog owner acts out departure routines by jingling keys, putting on a coat, and opening and closing a door without actually leaving. Practicing this can desensitize a dog to departure routines because he won't be able to associate them with being left alone. If you are unable to get your dog's separation anxiety under control, don't lose hope. A consultation with a trainer or canine behaviorist may result in an effective behavior modification plan.

Coprophagia (Stool Eating)

Stool eating is perhaps the most disturbing (to humans) behavior that a dog may develop. It's not clear why some dogs develop this habit and others don't. It could be a learned behavior. It could be caused by diet deficiency. Or it could be related to the cleanliness of the environment in which a puppy was raised. In any case, it can cause a lot of problems for your dog.

Ingesting his own feces or that of other animals can cause diarrhea and stomach upset, not to mention exposing your dog to internal parasites or diseases. This behavior usually begins in puppyhood and often diminishes by the time a puppy matures to about 18 months, so time eventually provides its own solution. The only problem, then, is determining how to manage this behavior until it is outgrown.

Managing Coprophagia

Help prevent your puppy's consumption of fecal material by keeping his outdoor areas clean and supervising him while outdoors. Diet supplements are readily available at pet supply stores that will make your puppy's feces unpalatable to him. For reasons unknown to veterinarians, some dogs who appear to have outgrown this habit suffer relapses during cold weather, but the behavior tends to diminish again when warmer seasons approach.

Older dogs who suddenly develop this habit should be checked by a veterinarian to see if health-related causes are responsible. Surgery, illness, and health conditions have been suspected of causing the development of this behavior in adult dogs.

Aggression

Dobermans are extremely loyal and trustworthy protectors. This is the job they have been bred to do for over a century. But some communities are embracing the trend to ban certain protective breeds. Some insurance companies now refuse to insure those who own certain breeds, and legislators are passing stricter laws and regulations concerning "vicious" dogs. The message is loud and clear: You do *not* want to own a dog who bites!

The difference between a protective dog and a vicious dog is that a protective dog will analyze a situation and use sound judgment before using his teeth, whereas a vicious dog will bite inappropriately and sometimes without warning or provocation. Dobermans can fall into either category, depending on their breeding, socialization, and training.

There are several different types of aggression, and each one is handled differently. Regardless of which type, *any* form of aggression is considered a very serious behavior issue, especially for Dobermans, because this particular breed can do significant damage with a bite.

Professional guidance should be sought in any case of aggression. In addition to behavior modification, anti-anxiety and anti-depressant medications have been shown to have positive effects on managing this behavior. Consultation with a certified veterinary behavior specialist is highly recommended.

Prevent the development of aggressive behavior by properly training and socializing your dog. In addition, neutering and spaying can reduce aggressive tendencies, especially in males.

Food Aggression

A food-aggressive dog will take a threatening stance or snap at anyone who approaches or comes near his food. This type of aggression may develop independently of any other form of aggression. For instance, the gentlest dog may not show any other signs of aggression except when it comes to his food. Dogs have a natural instinct to protect their food source; this is a necessary survival instinct. They begin competing for food with their littermates at a very young age. When this protectiveness results in aggression toward people, it becomes a problem.

Do not underestimate the seriousness of food aggression. It may seem like an innocuous behavior that is perfectly tolerable as long as you leave your dog alone when he's eating, but you are still at risk of facing an expensive lawsuit if your food-aggressive dog bites an unwary guest, or worse, injures an innocent child. *Any form of aggression should not be tolerated*.

Correcting Food Aggression

If your dog displays food-aggressive behavior, the first course of action should be to make sure your leadership status is clear by practicing basic obedience training. When your leadership is not in question, begin to teach your dog that you are his food source, and as such, you are in control of his food and have the right to take it away if he does not behave appropriately.

When you feed your dog, begin by feeding him a handful of food over his dish. If he shows any sign of aggression, close your hand and take the food away. As long as he doesn't show any sign of protectiveness, allow him to eat the rest of the food from your hand. Then give him the remainder of his meal in his dish, but make him sit and do not allow him to eat until you give him an *ok*. This will help desensitize your dog to having a hand near his food

Aggressive Biting

Aggressive biting is completely different from normal mouthing. If your puppy or dog bares his teeth or snaps at any person, ask your veterinarian or obedience instructor for a referral, and talk to a dog trainer or behaviorist who is qualified to evaluate the behavior and to deal with aggression. Don't wait—if your puppy is just very pushy, you must get control as soon as possible. If he's showing true aggression, it will not get better on its own and it could escalate, so get professional help.

dish and reinforce the message that you are in control.

If you feel you are unable to conduct this behavior modification technique safely, do not hesitate to consult a professional trainer or behaviorist. It is not worth risking injury to yourself by attempting to solve this problem alone.

Fear Aggression

Fear-aggressive dogs bite as a defensive reaction. They are insecure, fearful, shy, lack social skills, or may have been traumatized by abuse. They may be fearful of adults (particularly men, who are larger and louder than women), children, or other dogs, and biting is their way of attempting to control a situation. Fear aggression can be distinguished from dominance aggression by a dog's body posture, which is submissive or anxious: ears are back, head is held low, and the tail is held low or tucked between the legs.

Correcting Fear Aggression

The best thing you can do for a fear-aggressive dog is to help him gain some confidence, not only in himself, but also in you. A dog who has a trustworthy leader will feel less anxious and therefore feel less need to defend himself. You also need to be careful not to reward fearful behavior by petting and cuddling your dog in an effort to soothe him.

A trainer experienced with this type of aggression can help you develop a training program to address this problem. A behavior modification plan might include gradually desensitizing your dog to fearful stimulus and practicing obedience commands to establish control and confidence.

Dominance Aggression

Dominance aggression is perhaps the most serious form of aggression. A dog who does not learn his place among the household hierarchy may think he rules the roost. He can become possessive of toys, furniture, or even people whom he considers it his duty to protect. He may also become territorially aggressive.

Dominance, in combination with the Doberman's independent nature, can produce a volatile mixture. This is why professional help is imperative in solving dominance aggression in Dobermans.

Correcting Dominance Aggression

Obedience classes are a necessity, not an option, when it comes to learning how to control a dominant dog. But you also need to seek out a training instructor who has experience with dominant dogs. Contemporary training methods, although they are very effective with dogs who have a high will to please, are not always effective with a dog who is more interested in controlling you than pleasing you. A trainer versed in the correct training methods can help you cultivate your dog's will to please.

If territorial protectiveness becomes unmanageable or dangerous to you or to nonthreatening visitors, you may need professional help to find solutions.

Enforcing your status with a dominant dog also involves getting him off the furniture and letting him know who is in control of the food. If you previously allowed your dog on the bed or couch, it's time to teach him that his place is below you and on the floor. Coax him off the furniture with a food reward if necessary, and direct him to lie down on a blanket or dog bed. When feeding your dominant dog, always make him sit and wait for you to release him with an *ok* before allowing him to eat.

Dominant dogs always have to be reminded who is in control, and this affects how you handle your dog in almost every situation. This includes how you dole out praise, petting, and affection. If you are the type of person who loves to hug, hold, and cuddle your dog, and you are in the habit of lavishing him with petting and attention, you will have to practice some self-control in this area. Dominant dogs should only receive petting and praise when they have *earned* it. If your dog obeys commands, vacates the furniture willingly, or sits and waits nicely before feeding, he has earned physical or verbal attention. With the right training, handling, and expert assistance, a dominant dog will accept his proper rank and conform his behavior appropriately.

Territorial Aggression

One of the greatest advantages in owning a Doberman is the sense of security he provides. Knowing that your dog will defend

Problem Behaviors and Obedience Class

The severity of many problem behaviors often lessens as a result of general obedience training. If you haven't already done so, take your dog to a good obedience class now. Even if he doesn't exhibit the behavior in class, and you don't directly address the problem there, the training will improve communication between you and your dog. It will also make him more confident and secure, and he may not feel the need to engage in the problem behavior as often.

you and your property against unwanted intruders makes you feel safe in your own home and helps you sleep well at night. Protecting territory is a very natural canine behavior, and in the case of the Doberman, it is his inbred job to let you know of the approach of strangers or the breach of interlopers. But when this territorial protectiveness becomes extreme, unmanageable, or dangerous to nonthreatening visitors, it is a very serious problem.

Correcting Territorial Aggression

If your dog is nonaggressive toward people and other dogs on neutral territory away from home but becomes overly protective of your home or yard when he is at home, he is territorially aggressive. Territorial aggression can be a by-product of dominance aggression or fear aggression, the difference being determined by your dog's body posture. Territorial aggression related to dominance will put your dog in a confident, ears-forward posture.

In either case, your dog needs to learn to trust your judgment of a situation so that he will not feel a need to act on his own. Treatment will consist of establishing control and leadership through obedience training and implementing behavior modification techniques designed to desensitize and condition your dog to behave appropriately. Like other forms of aggression, this training should be done with the guidance of a professional trainer or behaviorist.

Precautions will also need to be taken to prevent accidental injuries until your dog can be trusted to react appropriately to stimulus that provokes aggressive behavior. A head halter or muzzle may be needed to keep him under control, doors and gates will need to be secured to prevent access to your property by unwary dogs or humans, constant outdoor supervision will be required, and a safe protocol for introducing visitors will need to be implemented.

SEEKING PROFESSIONAL HELP ▰▰▰

Thankfully, most canine problem behaviors can be prevented or solved with training and socialization, but there are always some situations you should not expect to handle on your own. Your veterinarian should be the first professional to consult because he can rule out health conditions as a cause of the inappropriate behavior. He can also refer you to a professional trainer, canine behaviorist, or a certified veterinary behavior specialist if one is available in your area.

Professional guidance for canine problem behaviors is often just a phone call away. Your local animal shelter may have an expert on staff who can provide valuable advice, and if not, he or she may be able to refer you to someone else who can help. Doberman breeders or rescue organizations have a lot of expertise they can share with you regarding your Doberman's behavior, and they are often more than happy to help a fellow owner of the breed.

Great strides have been made in the study of animal behavior in the last decade. Many veterinary schools have been devoting more research and resources to this subject. Professional trainers and animal shelters are doing their best to keep abreast of new behavior modification techniques, and those who specialize in animal behavior have realized the need to standardize techniques, establish ethics, and provide a way to ensure quality practices. This has been accomplished with the formation of animal behavior organizations in the United States and Great Britain.

The International Association of Animal Behavior Consultants (IAABC) in the United States and The Association of Pet Behaviour Counsellors (APBC) in Great Britain are great sources of information and referrals. Individuals who are certified through these organizations are required to have education and experience qualifications. Even so, you should evaluate animal behaviorists carefully. A good behaviorist will ask plenty of questions to qualify the problem and be able to indicate what kind of help she is able to provide. She should be knowledgeable about the particular problem you need to solve, and she should indicate her commitment to humane training methods.

There are more solutions to problem behaviors than ever before. With so many resources now available to dog owners, there is no reason to give up on a dog because of behavior issues. Help is out there, and this gives all of us more than solutions—it gives us hope.

Training is like a pyramid, with communication, understanding, and knowledge becoming stronger and more precise with each level, until it narrows to perfection at the top. How high will you climb? The amazingly obedient dog you envision could very well be the dog at your own feet!

7

ADVANCED TRAINING and ACTIVITIES

With Your Doberman Pinscher

Once you have discovered how fun and rewarding it is to train your dog, you might begin to look at him in a different light. Dobermans are wonderful companions and protectors, but they can also be a joy with which to share a variety of activities and sports. All you need is your dog and a little time for ongoing training.

Training is a learning experience, a social experience, and an activity that can keep both you and your dog healthy and active. If you enjoy spending time with your dog, this is the most productive and beneficial way to do it. Moreover, by doing so, you will gain a greater mutual understanding and develop a stronger bond.

INTELLIGENCE AND LEARNING

Intelligence alone does not determine how quickly your dog will learn new skills. If you have gone a number of years without schooling and then decided to take a few classes, you've noticed how difficult it is to get back into the habit of learning. Dogs are the same way. Even a dog of average intelligence will begin to learn new tasks more quickly if he is constantly challenged to do so.

Dobermans, having exceptional intelligence to begin with, will amaze you with their learning capacity if their minds are kept active. So never stop training your dog. Don't call it quits after he has learned basic obedience and household manners. Always keep your mind open to the possibilities and think of new, useful, or fun things to teach him. Training is a great way to spend time with your dog and develop a unique relationship with him, and the skills he learns will impress everyone who meets him.

Even if you do not participate in formal obedience classes or compete in any of a number of training disciplines, you can borrow skills from these activities to keep your dog mentally active. Every moment you spend in training improves communication with your dog and increases his responsiveness to you, resulting in that amazingly attentive and wonderfully obedient dog of your dreams!

THE CANINE GOOD CITIZEN® TEST

The Canine Good Citizen (CGC) Certification program sponsored by the American Kennel Club (AKC) is one of the best training opportunities available for dog owners who want to go a step beyond basic obedience. This program was started in 1989 as a way to include all dog owners in the activities of the AKC, to promote responsible dog ownership, and to emphasize the canine contribution to our communities.

The skills needed to pass the CGC test demonstrate your control of your dog, your dog's manners in public, and your attitude toward responsible dog ownership. Although the skills are rather simple in nature, they do require practice and the development of self-control. Many training facilities offer classes devoted to teaching CGC skills, but only evaluators approved by the AKC can perform testing and certification. You can locate these evaluators by checking with local training facilities or contacting the AKC for referrals.

The Canine Good Citizen program encourages owners to foster and encourage good manners in their dogs.

The value of a well-trained, well-mannered dog has not gone unrecognized. Thirty-four states have now enacted CGC resolutions; some insurance companies are willing to waive liability restrictions for dogs who have obtained CGC certification; and many institutions, such as schools, nursing homes, and hospitals, now accept canine visitors who have passed the CGC test. Hotels and other places of business are often willing to make exceptions to their no-pets policies for CGC graduates. And a number of organizations have incorporated CGC training as part of their own programs, such as 4-H and Therapy Dogs International.

The CGC is an especially worthy goal for Doberman owners because it helps to promote a positive image of the breed. There is no better way to dispel the myths and misconceptions about the breed than to exhibit your dog publicly as a good canine citizen. Overall, CGC-certified dogs are more readily accepted as a part of mainstream society because they are trained to behave appropriately in the human world, and this type of training can create an even stronger foundation for all other types of training.

ADVANCED OBEDIENCE TRAINING

It's nice to have a dog schooled in basic obedience, but if you really want a reliable and responsive dog, advanced obedience training can help you reach a whole new level of human-to-dog communication. Whether your goal is to improve your dog's basic obedience skills or to eventually compete in obedience trials, advanced training classes are the best way to pursue higher canine education. The distractions of learning in the company of other dogs cannot be duplicated at home, and the guidance of a professional trainer is always well worth the investment.

Intermediate Training Classes

Intermediate training classes are designed to perfect your dog's skills in basic obedience by providing additional practice. They will also help him develop attention skills and provide distractions to help improve his reliability. Your dog will be required to perform certain skills for longer time periods, and he will learn a few new skills to add to his repertoire, like heeling, out-of-sight stay, drop-on-recall, and off-leash work. Intermediate classes are a prerequisite if you are interested in obedience competition, but they can also be a worthwhile hobby if you truly want a superb pet.

Advanced Training Classes

Advanced training classes are more demanding. They focus on teaching skills necessary to compete in advanced obedience trials. Some of the skills covered include retrieving, directed jumping, hand signals, and scent discrimination, which requires the dog to determine which item in a group of objects bears his owner's scent. The curriculum for these classes is often flexible, depending on the specific needs of the class participants, so inquire as to the format of any advanced training class to make sure it will cover the areas you wish to work on.

After the highest level of advanced training class is completed, you and your dog will hopefully know all the skills you need to

AKC Canine Good Citizen® Test

Test 1: Accepting a friendly stranger

Test 2: Sitting politely for petting

Test 3: Appearance and grooming

Test 4: Out for a walk

Test 5: Walking through a crowd

Test 6: *Sit* and *down* on command; staying in place

Test 7: Coming when called

Test 8: Reaction to another dog

Test 9: Reaction to distractions

Test 10: Supervised separation

To receive the CGC certificate, dogs must pass all 10 items of the test.

Note: Evaluators may withhold the CGC certificate if a significant incident is observed (e.g., dog bites a person or another dog) in the immediate testing area.

Source: The AKC Canine Good Citizen® Test Evaluation Form

compete in obedience trials. But how do you keep your dog's skills in top form? Practicing at home, as stated earlier, will not provide the distractions necessary to guarantee a good performance at competition. Many training facilities offer weekly practice sessions called obedience run-thrus, which can give you the chance to practice in a competition-like setting.

Obedience Trials

If you have never had the opportunity to observe an obedience trial at an AKC-sponsored event, it is highly recommended that you do so. You will be immediately impressed with the level of skill and precision executed by the dogs, as well as the relationship they have with their handlers. The experience may inspire you, as it has so many others, to take a stab at this rewarding dog sport.

Competition is divided into different skill levels, which gives you the opportunity to compete at an early stage of training while providing incentives for you to advance to more difficult levels. This keeps participation high and motivation strong.

Levels of Competition

Whatever your reasons for continuing to train, working regularly with your Doberman will strengthen the bond between you, direct his energy in a positive way, and help keep him fit and trim.

The Novice level of competition, which offers the Companion Dog (CD) title, will require skills such as come, staying with a group of dogs, heeling on and off leash, and standing for examination.

The Open level, which leads to the Companion Dog Excellent (CDX) title, challenges dogs by requiring them to perform some skills for longer periods of time and adding additional skills, like retrieving and jumping.

The Utility level, which is rewarded with a Utility Dog (UD) title, is the most interesting obedience event to observe. It includes directed jumping, directed retrieving, and scent discrimination. Dogs who obtain this title may go on to earn the Utility Dog Excellent (UDX) title if they perform consistently at the Utility level.

There is no end of the trail in obedience competition. Even those dogs who obtain a UDX title can continue to compete at the Utility level to obtain the prestigious Obedience Trial Champion title (OTCH). There are many opportunities to compete in obedience, and your success is limited only by the time you put into it and your drive to succeed.

THERAPY DOG WORK

Therapy dog work is one of the most positive ways you can have fun with your Doberman and contribute to your community at the same time. The concept of using dogs as emotional support for the elderly and infirm began in the 1970s when Elaine Smith, an American registered nurse working in England, noticed how patients benefited from interacting with animals. She returned to the United States and founded Therapy Dogs International, Inc. (TDI) in 1976, which continues to certify, insure, and register therapy dogs in the United States, Canada, and other countries.

Requirements for a Good Therapy Dog

The Doberman definitely has much to offer in the line of therapy work. His size makes him easy to reach from wheelchairs and beds, and his short, clean coat is desirable for health care settings. But this does not mean that all Dobermans are qualified for the task. Temperament and training are exceedingly more important than physical characteristics. A therapy dog must be well socialized, calm, controlled, and friendly.

Provided that your dog has the right qualifications, you might consider enrolling him in a therapy dog training class offered by a local training facility. Be sure to check if certification will be awarded upon completion of the class, or if testing is conducted separately. Basic obedience training will be a prerequisite for therapy dog training.

Requirements for a Good Therapy Dog Owner

Qualifications are not restricted to your dog because you will also need to meet certain criteria. You have to be willing to commit the time and effort to this activity; patients look forward to regular, consistent visits and will be disappointed if you are chronically late or don't show up when you are scheduled to visit. You will have to learn how to interact appropriately with staff and patients,

Health Benefits of Canine Companionship

Studies have shown that interaction with animals can reduce stress and tension, lower blood pressure, improve morale, and result in quicker recoveries from illness or surgery. The results of these studies have been so inspiring that therapy dog work has expanded beyond nursing home and hospital visits to include mental health facilities, rehabilitation facilities, schools, and prisons. It has also given birth to many local and national organizations that support therapy dog use.

Search and Rescue Credentials

Search and rescue handlers are volunteers who must be willing to commit considerable time and resources. They must also be physically fit, love working outside, and enjoy working with their dogs. Necessary equipment, which they will often need to supply themselves, includes working harnesses, long lines, safety vests and protective boots for the dogs, radios, flashlights, hard hat, compass, and a pack to carry items on the trail. Handlers should also become certified in cardiopulmonary resuscitation and first aid, and their dogs must become proficient in a number of disciplines, including obedience, agility, retrieving, and tracking. It may take a year or longer to sufficiently train a dog to perform all the necessary skills, so this is an activity reserved only for the most capable dogs and equally dedicated handlers.

become familiar with facility rules, adhere to safety practices, and be prepared to deal with inappropriate handling of your dog by residents or patients.

Getting Started

There are two ways to get started in this activity. You can obtain your Doberman's therapy dog certification and approach facilities in your area to see if they could use your services. Or, you can join a local therapy dog group that can provide support and resources for your endeavor. The latter is a good choice if you wish to gain additional training in the company of others who are more experienced. It can also give you the opportunity to conduct visits with other dog and handler teams rather than operating alone. You can locate an organization in your area by visiting the Therapy Dogs Inc. website at www.therapydogs.com, which has a comprehensive database of these organizations.

SEARCH AND RESCUE

Another very worthy volunteer activity for you and your Doberman is search-and-rescue work. It requires an adventurous spirit, a strong constitution, and a considerable commitment of time and resources, but the benefits are enormous. There is no greater joy than finding a lost child or bringing closure to those who have lost a loved one. And there is no doubt the Doberman has what it takes to excel at it; he has energy, perseverance, and an unquestionable talent for tracking.

Most of us were awestruck by the valiant efforts of the search-and-rescue dogs who worked tirelessly with their handlers at ground zero after 9/11. But heroism does not come easily or without expense. Search-and-rescue dog handlers are required to commit a considerable amount of time to training and practice each week. They are often expected to provide their own equipment and supplies, which may include hard hats, safety vests, and protective boots for their dogs. They may also have to arrange for their own transportation to search-and-rescue sites, all without the benefit of financial compensation.

Getting Started

Training your dog for search-and-rescue work involves developing proficiency in a number of disciplines, including obedience, agility, retrieving, and tracking. It may take a year or longer to sufficiently train your dog to perform all the necessary skills, so this is an activity reserved only for the most capable dogs and equally dedicated handlers.

In addition to the skills expected of your dog, you need to meet certain requirements yourself, including being physically fit enough to handle the demands of the job, having knowledge of wilderness survival skills or collapsed building safety, and learning how to operate in a cooperative effort with other dog handlers, police, medical, or other emergency personnel.

This is definitely not a job for the faint of heart—it often involves recovering human remains—but it is a very important job that needs to be done nonetheless. If you are so inspired to make the commitment, the National Association for Search and Rescue (NASAR) can put you in touch with a group in your area. More information is available at their website at www.nasar.org.

SHOWING YOUR DOG

You have the most beautiful dog in *Doberdom*, and this isn't just your pride speaking. You have studied the Doberman breed standard and sought expert advice in choosing an excellent show-quality dog. Now you want to show him off to the world!

Many rewards can be gained in the sport of dog showing. Besides the possibility of winning an award, showing provides an opportunity to show off your canine pride and joy, to promote the Doberman breed by sharing your expertise with show-goers, and to fraternize with other exhibitors. Can you think of anything more fun to do with your dog on a weekend?

Conformation competitions focus on the physical and temperament qualities of your dog and compare them to the applicable breed standard. Dogs who come closest to meeting their breed standard are awarded, and this can result in more than a nice trophy or ribbon to hang on the wall. It can significantly increase the value of your dog as breeding stock.

Getting Started

Getting started in showing actually begins before you acquire your dog. You should attend as many dog shows as possible to become familiar with how they are organized. Speak to exhibitors, study the Doberman breed standard thoroughly, and seek expert advice in choosing a show dog prospect. The more you know ahead of time, the better your chances for success.

Showing dogs can be an expensive endeavor. You will need to purchase the correct equipment, such as a show collar, lead, and grooming supplies. There are entry fees and travel expenses to consider, as well as fees for a professional handler if you choose to hire one. All of this can add up to quite a tally, so be prepared for the costs. If you strive to earn a championship as quickly as possible, you will incur considerable expenses traveling to shows out of state. But if you limit yourself to a few local shows each year and participate more for the fun of it, you will have fewer expenses.

Training Your Dog for Showing

Dogs are not born knowing how to perform well in a show. They must be taught how to walk and trot in a controlled manner and stand patiently for grooming and examinations. Dog shows are noisy, bustling places that can easily distract a dog out of civil behavior, so training is necessary to acclimate him to this environment and teach him how to behave appropriately. Basic obedience instruction is a must, and continuing education in a conformation class should be in your plans. These classes are not difficult to find; they are offered at most training facilities and also by some Doberman clubs.

At a dog show, dogs are judged against the standard for the breed.

People, likewise, are not born knowing how to conduct themselves in the show ring. Conformation training classes are a good education for you as well as your dog. They can teach you how to fit and operate a show collar, how to carry the leash, and how to walk and jog alongside your dog to show him to his best advantage.

Perfection comes with practice, and there is no better way to practice than to try your hand at a fun match. Various organizations and businesses sponsor dog shows that are not sanctioned by the AKC. Although points and titles are not awarded, valuable experience can be gained. These shows often feature many young dogs and novice handlers getting their first show experience under their belts. Check with your local Doberman club or local pet supply businesses to find out when and where these events are being held.

Professional Handlers

If you are not confident enough to show your own dog, a professional handler can do it for you. Professional handler fees vary depending on the work they do. If they are required to train your dog or provide grooming services, the cost will be higher. Breeders and Doberman clubs are the best sources for referrals, but keep in mind that dogs, as well as people, are individuals. Some dogs perform better for their owners and others perform best in the hands of a professional.

Show Grooming

The plus side of showing a Doberman is that it doesn't involve as much intensive grooming as preparing a curly-coated or long-haired breed for show. There are some tricks of the trade—knowing which shampoos to use to enhance the color of your dog, how to touch up minor coat imperfections, and how to trim the nails short enough to meet show expectations—but these can be learned by observing and consulting with other exhibitors, breeders, or Doberman club members. In most cases, it is not necessary to hire a professional groomer unless your dog has met with an extremely bad hair day experience, such as getting tarred or skunked the day before a show.

Entering the Dog Show

To enter a dog show, you must first find out when and where shows are being held. The AKC and KC maintain event schedules on their websites and also publish this information in their respective publications, the *AKC Gazette* and the *Kennel Gazette*. *Premium Lists*, which include show dates, locations, entry information, deadlines, and show rules, are also available by subscription from these organizations.

Your dog must be entered in the correct class to avoid disqualification, so review the classes offered in each show to determine those in which he is eligible to compete. Then, be sure to send in the entry form and fee by the deadline.

What Is a Fun Match?

Fun matches are dog shows that are not sanctioned by the AKC and that do not provide points toward championships. They provide an opportunity for novice exhibitors and young dogs to gain show experience.

Judging

Dogs are initially judged in a class of their peers where they compete against other Dobermans of the same age and sex. The winners then go on to compete against winners of other Doberman classes until the top male and female are eventually chosen to contend against each other. The winner of this final Doberman contest is titled the Best of Winners and has the opportunity to vie against the top dogs of other breeds for the coveted title of Best in Show.

A judge will evaluate your dog in a couple of ways. She will want to inspect his physical conformation so she can compare it to the breed standard, and she will analyze his movement at a trot to determine how well his conformation conforms to function. You will be asked to stack your dog, which is to put him in a standing position so that the judge can get an up-close look at him. The judge will check his teeth, possibly run her hands lightly over parts of his body, and will also be mindful of how he responds to this handling.

To evaluate your dog's movement, the judge will ask you to trot him so she can observe his movement as he moves toward her or away from her, and she will also want to view his movement from the side. All the dogs in the class may conduct this activity at the same time, or you may be asked to do it individually. The judge always decides the exact sequence of activities.

Judging is not an exact science. You may find that your dog shows better under some judges than others. Every judge has to rely on his or her own knowledge and experience, but there is no avoiding the fact that judging involves formulating an opinion, and opinions aren't always shared by everybody. But there is one thing you can do to sway opinion in your favor when competition is close, and that is to show a positive attitude!

If you take showing too seriously and perform with a stone-faced expression, it will dull the visual appeal and performance of your dog. Smiling and having fun, on the other hand, will reflect in your dog's attitude and ultimately the judge's opinion. Showing isn't necessarily about winning (although winning is nice); it's about doing something you enjoy.

Eligibility for Conformation Competition

The main purpose of showing is to recognize dogs who possess superior qualities. These qualities would have little value if they could not be reproduced, which is why neutered or spayed dogs are not allowed in conformation competition. This is perhaps the biggest consideration in choosing to show your dog because intact dogs are a little more work to maintain than sterilized pets. As long as your Doberman is at least six months old, is a registered purebred, and does not possess a disqualifying fault, he will be eligible to compete in American Kennel Club (AKC) or Kennel Club (KC) sanctioned shows.

DOG SPORTS

Dobermans are athletic and vigorous canines who are perfectly suited to a number of dog sports that require agility, strength, and stamina. They love having a job to do, and you are sure to be impressed with your own Doberman's tenacity in any sport in which you choose to participate. Whether you endeavor to compete, or just seek to have some fun and get some exercise, he will likely put his heart and soul into it.

Agility

If you like speed, color, and excitement, agility is a sport that is packed with pure adrenaline. Fast-paced, challenging, and requiring a great deal of skill, agility provides a good aerobic workout for dogs and an entertaining spectacle for observers. No wonder it has become such a popular activity for canine sport enthusiasts!

The sport consists of a timed obstacle course your dog must traverse at your direction. The dog who completes the course the fastest and most accurately wins. The obstacles themselves often resemble those used to train police or military dogs. Various jumps and tunnels are combined with an A-frame, dog walk, see-saw, and pause table to provide an array of challenges.

Getting Started

Dobermans are obviously physically and mentally equipped for the demands of this sport, but it does take a considerable amount of training to prepare for competition. Most dog-training facilities offer classes to get started in agility, and a good number of books are available on the subject.

The rules and obstacles for each course vary depending on the particular competition and the organization sanctioning

Agility is a fast-paced sport that requires speed and coordination.

it. In the United States, agility competitions are sanctioned by several organizations including the American Kennel Club (AKC), the United Kennel Club (UKC), the North American Dog Agility Council (NADAC), and Canine Performance Events (CPE). In Great Britain, all agility competitions are governed by the Kennel Club (KC). Any one of these organizations is a good source of information and event schedules.

If you are not the competitive sort, agility can still become a fine activity for your energetic Doberman. Many people enjoy doing agility exercises in their own backyards by constructing or purchasing their own obstacles. There is no better way to keep your dog fit and get some fresh air at the same time.

Flyball

Flyball is another fast-paced dog sport that requires speed and coordination. The course is much simpler than the one used for agility trials and requires less training effort, but there is an added element of teamwork. A team consists of four dogs who must run a relay-type race. Each dog runs a straight 51-foot (15.5-m) course over several hurdles to retrieve a ball from a ball launcher at the end of the course. A ball is released when the dog presses a pedal on the front of the ball launcher box, and the dog is required to bring the ball back through the course to his handler. The next dog on the team is then released to run the course, and so forth, until all four dogs complete the course for a total time score. Missed jumps or dropped balls, of course, result in penalties.

The sport was initially the brainchild of Herbert Wagner, who constructed the first tennis ball launcher used in his obedience classes in the 1970s. A demonstration on *The Tonight Show* caught the attention of other dog trainers, and it later became a viable sport with the formation of the North American Flyball Association (NAFA) in 1985. NAFA now regulates flyball tournaments in North America, Europe, and other regions. Tournaments are organized so that teams with similar abilities compete against each other. This keeps competition fair and fun for everyone.

Getting Started

Dobermans with a strong prey drive (desire to chase moving objects) or a real fetish for fetching are great prospects for this sport. You don't need to be an expert in canine body language to see that the dogs who participate in this sport enjoy it immensely. And what's fun for the dogs is fun for their owners!

If you are interested in learning more about flyball, a cyber trip to the NAFA website at www.flyball.org can give you information on local flyball clubs. You can also check training facilities in your area for flyball training classes.

Freestyle

Canine musical freestyle is a relatively new dog sport that continues to grow and evolve. Its greatest appeal, perhaps, is the music, which adds an upbeat mood to a very unique obedience demonstration. Colorful costumes, themes, and humor have been added to this sport to make it one of the most interesting and entertaining dog sports in recent history.

Also called "dog dancing" or "heelwork to music," canine musical freestyle evolved from several demonstrations in the United States and Great Britain between 1989 and 1990, but it was a performance involving a troupe of dogs and handlers at the Pacific Canine Showcase in British Columbia, Canada, in 1991 that brought freestyle to a larger public audience. The performance generated so much interest that the first freestyle competition was held at the Pacific Canine Showcase the following year.

The formation of Musical Canine Sports International (MCSI) followed shortly after to establish standardized judging criteria, and the sport has continued to blossom ever since. A number of organizations now sanction freestyle events, some preferring to focus on the traditional obedience aspect of the sport and others branching off to promote its entertainment value. The most interesting and creative expressions of freestyle incorporate costumes and unique maneuvers that are more accurately described as tricks rather than obedience skills.

In the United Kingdom, Canine Freestyle GB and the Paws N Music Association have made it their responsibility to promote and provide guidance in the sport of freestyle. In the United States, the World Canine Freestyle Organization (WCFO), Canine Freestyle Federation (CFF), Paws2Dance, and the Musical Dog Sport Association (MDSA) are the leading authorities.

A Silly Concept Becomes an Impressive Sport

The concept of dancing with a dog might seem silly at first. Sure, it's fun to participate in and amusing to watch, but to gain a true appreciation of canine musical freestyle, consider the fact that freestyle dogs need to learn a minimum of 20 different commands and maneuvers to perform a routine (this requires more skills than advanced obedience competition!). It's not unheard of for an advanced dog to execute 40 or more different maneuvers. Add in the choreography and the challenge of moving to the beat of music, and you can see how much really goes into this sport. If you have never witnessed a freestyle demonstration, be prepared to be impressed!

Everyday Sports

Dobermans are wonderful companions and protectors, but they can also be a joy with which to share a variety of activities and sports. Getting off the couch to spend time with our dogs keeps us active and provides social opportunities, nurturing both our physical and emotional well-being. More importantly, you will gain a greater mutual understanding and develop a stronger bond.

Getting Started

Dobermans, always at the top of the class in obedience competitions, are excellent prospects for this new and fun form of obedience training. Many training facilities now offer freestyle classes for those interested in pursuing the sport, and competition need not be one of your goals. Freestyle is an impressive display of teamwork between dog and handler and can make a wonderfully amusing demonstration for entertainment purposes. For more information on this unique canine activity, see the WCFO website at www.worldcaninefreestyle.org.

Tracking

Tracking is a sport that demonstrates a dog's amazing scenting ability. A dog's olfactory capability is 100,000 times that of a human, and this natural talent has been used to serve mankind in a number of situations, including locating lost individuals or fugitives and detecting drugs, bombs, accelerants, or deadly molds. In AKC tracking events, the dog's ability to follow a human scent trail is put to the test.

A tracklayer maps out a trail with several turns and leaves a number of articles—gloves, clothing, wallets, or other items—along the trail for the dog to find. The test for the dog is relatively simple: He must follow the trail and locate the items to pass the test. If he loses the trail and doesn't find all the items, he fails the test.

Dobermans fare quite well at tracking events because they have the drive to pursue a trail to its conclusion. Tracking is a job they embrace with gusto, which is why they make such good prospects for police work, search and rescue, and other types of work that involve scenting.

If you enjoy exercise and spending time outdoors with your dog, tracking could be the dog sport for you. But it can be a physically demanding activity. The trail may include obstacles like streams or logs to cross, and the weather is always at the whim of nature. Tracking events are rarely cancelled due to weather conditions.

Levels of Competition

If you have the ambition to pursue this sport, your efforts may be rewarded with a title for your dog. Your dog can earn the Tracking Dog (TD) title by completing a track of 440 to 500 yards (402 to 457 m) that includes three to five changes of direction and an article to be located at the end. This trail is aged up to two hours before your dog will be allowed to begin scenting.

Once a TD title is obtained, you are allowed to pursue a Tracking Dog Excellent (TDX) title, which involves scenting a trail 800 to 1,000 yards (732 to 914 m) long with five to seven changes of direction and three articles left along the track for your dog to find. The track is aged up to five hours, and cross tracks are used as diversions to make the course more challenging.

TDX dogs can go on to earn a Variable Surface Tracking (VST) title. The most challenging test of all, it includes a track of 600 to 800 yards (549 to 732 m) with four to eight changes of direction. The track is aged up to five hours and includes tracking over different surfaces, such as concrete, and locating four items made of dissimilar materials (leather, plastic, fabric, and metal). The cream of the crop in tracking events, which are the dogs who have obtained all three tracking titles, are automatically awarded a Champion Tracker (CT) title.

Getting Started

Getting involved in tracking begins with enrolling in a training class offered at a local training facility or through a tracking club. The AKC maintains a list of tracking clubs that can be accessed through its website at www.akc.org. When you are ready to compete, check their schedule of events to find out when and where tracking events are being held.

The sport of Schutzhund evaluates and tests a dog's skills in performing the tasks a working dog is bred to do: obedience, tracking, and protection.

Schutzhund

Schutzhund is a German word for "protection dog." The sport of Schutzhund evaluates and tests a dog's skills in performing the tasks a working dog is bred to do: obedience, tracking, and protection. Started in Germany in 1903, Schutzhund tests were designed to evaluate a dog's suitability as a working dog and to help breeders choose the best dogs for breeding. It was initially a sport that focused on police dogs, but it eventually gained the interest of private citizens who sought a better level of personal protection.

Three levels of competition lead to the titles of Schutzhund I, Schutzhund II, and Schutzhund III, with each level becoming progressively more difficult. Schutzhund I requires obedience skills such as heeling on and off leash and retrieving on the flat and over a hurdle. The dog must be at least 18 months old and able to follow a track at least 20 minutes old laid by his owner. Certain protection tests are also included. As you can see, even the first leg of Schutzhund competition is not a realistic goal for beginners. Training in advanced obedience, tracking, and protection are required.

Schutzhund II is open to dogs 19 months and older who have already obtained their Schutzhund I title. The tests are the same as Schutzhund I but are more challenging and require greater agility and control. A retrieve over a 6-foot (1.8-m) slanted wall is added, and the track is laid by a stranger and aged at least 30 minutes.

The highest honor, Schutzhund III, is reserved for dogs at least 20 months old who have already earned Schutzhund I and Schutzhund II titles. Exercises in obedience and protection are all conducted off leash, and the track is older and more complicated. Protection skills are quite advanced, with the dog required to search for a "villain," hold him at bay, and prevent an assault on his handler, all while remaining under his handler's complete control. A dog worthy of this title is the ultimate working dog.

Getting Started

Although Dobermans appear to be perfectly suited to this sport, this does not mean that every Doberman is a good candidate. A Doberman who competes for Schutzhund titles must have an exceptionally stable temperament, without the excitability that sometimes comes with a high-energy dog. In fact, dogs must first be temperament tested by a judge before being allowed to compete. In a preliminary level of Schutzhund, called the B (or the BH or VB), obedience skills are tested and a thorough temperament test is conducted.

This is a sport for those who are serious about training and committed to following through on teaching the skills necessary to obtain a title. Because the protection aspect of Schutzhund involves teaching your dog how, when, and where to bite, an incorrectly or partially trained Doberman can be exceptionally dangerous. Dogs who receive the correct and complete course of training, on the other hand, will exercise the utmost in self-discipline and control when fulfilling their protective duties, and they are considered to be safer than those who receive no training at all.

If you are interested in participating in this challenging sport, invest the time in learning as much as possible before getting your feet wet. Observe Schutzhund competitions, speak to competitors, and read books devoted to the subject. The German organization that governs Schutzhund competitions worldwide, the DVG (Deutscher Berband der Gebrauchshundsportvereine), offers valuable information on their American-based website, www.dvgamerica.com. This site will give event information on Schutzhund trials and training clubs in your area.

OUTDOOR ACTIVITIES

Do you feel guilty about leaving your dog at home when you leave the house? Does he gaze after you with sorrowful eyes that plead, "Can't I come along?" Well, there are plenty of opportunities for you to invite your dog to come with you! Whether you want to get some exercise or just want to spend more time with your dog, there are lots of activities to suit you both.

Sports and Safety

Canine sports, like human sports, involve some risk of physical injury. Taking steps to avoid accidents allows you and your dog to continue enjoying the many benefits of canine activities. The following precautions should be observed while practicing or competing in any canine sport:

- Always check your training and sport equipment prior to practice or competition to make sure everything is in good repair and operating correctly. This includes jumps, obstacles, and even collars and leashes.

- Keep your dog in good physical shape with regular practice and exercise. Do not encourage your dog to overexert himself, even if he seems to have the will and drive to work indefinitely.

- Postpone or cancel practices or competitions if your dog displays any signs of soreness or illness. If your dog is not in top condition, he will be more prone to injuries. Health conditions may worsen, or he may spread illness to other dogs.

- Always bring a canine first-aid kit with you to any canine sport event.

- Seek veterinary attention immediately if your dog is injured while practicing or competing. Treating injuries professionally and promptly will get your dog back in top form quickly, while ignoring injuries may result in permanent damage that will exclude your dog from future competition.

When dogs are given an adequate amount of recreation time, they are healthier, happier, and better behaved.

Hiking

Hiking is great exercise for you and your dog. Your Doberman is endowed with enough stamina and endurance to handle just about any length hike you care to master, so if you enjoy fresh air and the outdoors, take your dog with you for a nice long walk.

Hiking does not need to be a wilderness experience. You can hike with your dog just about anywhere, but safety precautions should be observed just the same. Be mindful of weather conditions that can cause frostbite, hypothermia, or heat exhaustion. Road salt can irritate the pads of your dog's feet, and extreme heat can make sand or asphalt hot enough to burn them. Your Doberman's thin coat makes him more susceptible to weather conditions and also makes him more prone to scratches and injuries from heavy brush. Plan your hikes to avoid such hazards, and be sure to take a basic first aid kit with you. Antibiotic ointment, sterile wound dressings, vet wrap, and tweezers for removing splinters and thorns should be included.

Other necessary items to take along include drinking water, a water dish, rags or wipes, and dog waste bags. Depending on the length, purpose, and destination of your hike, you may want to bring some dog toys, a tie-out leash, and something for you and your dog to eat. By now you're probably wondering how you're going to carry all this stuff.

A backpack or waist pack is best for hiking because it will not interfere with your walking style. But why should you bear the entire burden? Some backpacks are made specifically with your dog in mind. Get one that is well fitted and preferably fleece-lined. Any chafing against your Doberman's sleek coat is likely to rub the hair off down to the skin. If you prepare adequately for your hikes, they can be enjoyable journeys for both you and your dog.

Jogging

Your Doberman would love nothing more than to join you on a jog. The exhilaration of trotting at your side and exploring the scenery in your neighborhood is wonderful stimulation and a great outlet for his limitless energy. Be sure to teach your dog how to travel on a loose leash first so that your jogging expedition doesn't turn into a tug of war. Afterward, you can tie the leash around your waist or purchase a belt specifically designed to hold the leash while you jog. This will free your arms so you can jog comfortably.

Just as with hiking, be wary of footing hazards and weather conditions that can harm your dog. The added benefit of jogging with a Doberman is the security he provides while engaging in this activity. It is unlikely anyone will attempt to assail you with your personal bodyguard by your side!

Cycling

Dobermans make excellent cycling partners, and as with hiking and jogging, joining you in this activity is another great opportunity for them to burn up some of that huge reservoir of energy. Even though they are made for endurance, they will obviously expend more energy running alongside a bicycle than you will from pedaling it. Don't overwork your dog, and gauge your speed and distance so you don't overdo it.

The greatest hazard in cycling with a dog is the potential for a bad wreck if the dog attempts to run in front of the bike or gets caught in the wheels. The proper safety equipment can prevent this type of accident. A bike attachment is available from pet supply stores and catalogs that will hold the leash to keep your dog at an adequate distance from your bike. It also allows your hands to be free for bike operation. Dog boots are also a good investment to protect your dog's feet from broken glass or other roadside debris.

This activity is best done along quieter roads or bike paths that do not present the hazard of congested or fast-moving traffic, gravel shoulders, or obstructions. Check out your route carefully before asking your dog to join you.

There are endless possibilities when it comes to training your dog. You can combine your own interests with the particular talents of your Doberman so that you can both enjoy a fun activity together. Whether you want to volunteer for a worthy effort, earn some awards, or get some exercise, training and other activities are not just a matter of including your dog in your life, they're also a way to include yourself in his.

HEALTH

of Your Doberman Pinscher

B y now, it's obvious your Doberman requires a considerable investment on your part. You need to invest in healthy food and supplies to care for him. You need to invest the time to groom him, give him adequate exercise, and train him to be a good pet. You hope the creature you have lavished with love and proper care will live a long, happy life by your side! Health care is the best insurance for your investment. Regular checkups, vaccinations, and prompt treatment of illnesses and injuries will not only preserve your dog's longevity, they will also provide a better quality of life for him well into his senior years.

CHOOSING A VETERINARIAN

Most veterinarians are highly competent in providing excellent health care for dogs, but you still want to scrutinize them carefully before choosing the one with whom you can feel the most comfortable and confident. Your search for the right veterinarian begins with investigating veterinary clinics nearest your home because you don't want to drive a long distance in the case of a time-critical emergency.

Ask neighbors, friends, and coworkers who they would recommend and why. Your breeder or local Doberman rescue organization might be able to put you in touch with a veterinarian who has expertise in the specific health conditions commonly found in the breed. For example, if you choose to crop your dog's ears, it is especially important to find a veterinarian experienced in this highly specialized procedure.

When you have obtained a referral, a phone call to the vet's office will allow you to investigate further. Some questions to ask include:

- **What kind of specialized equipment does the clinic possess?** Some clinics are fully equipped with ultrasound equipment, modern anesthesia equipment, X-ray facilities, and laboratories. If the clinic is well equipped, it will prevent the possibility that you will be referred to another clinic or lab to obtain these services, but be prepared to pay higher fees for routine care. The goal is to locate a clinic that can provide a variety of services at the most reasonable rates.

Vet Care for Senior Dogs

When your dog reaches about eight years of age, start him on a preventive health care program designed for older dogs. This includes a complete physical checkup twice a year, including a dental exam. The vet will be able to detect any significant physical changes, look for signs of illness, and make sure that your dog is current on all necessary inoculations.

Ask if your older dog should be started on a special diet. Pet food manufacturers have developed senior formula blends of dry and canned food. Based on your dog's overall health, your vet may recommend adding vitamin or mineral supplements to his food. They will help to boost the immune system as well as help the body absorb nutrients.

If you have any questions about your dog's health care needs as he ages, speak with your vet. She may make recommendations regarding lifestyle changes that could benefit him in his senior years.

- **Do any of the veterinarians specialize in particular fields of study?** Some veterinarians have received additional education in holistic treatment methods, including chiropractic, acupuncture, or homeopathy. Others may be certified as animal behavior specialists and can help with serious behavior issues. Also, if you have other pets, it is important to find a clinic or animal hospital that can take care of the needs of all the species that reside in your home. If any of these specialties are important to you, they should be considered in making your choice.

- **What fees are charged for common health procedures such as vaccinations and sterilization surgery?** Veterinary care is a necessity, but it is also a part of the free enterprise system and subject to competition. In urban areas where there is an abundance of veterinary clinics from which to choose, it doesn't hurt to compare prices. Even though clinics that offer specialized equipment, after-hours care, or veterinarians with educational specialties may have a higher fee scale, this can all figure into making a sound decision.

- **What are the clinic's hours, and do they offer after-hours emergency care?** Obviously, if a clinic has hours that conflict with your work schedule, it will be difficult to do business with them. If a clinic does not offer after-hours emergency care, do they refer their clients to another facility? If so, is this facility within a short driving distance?

Finding a clinic or animal hospital you believe will meet your expectations is only the first step in securing excellent health care for your Doberman. The next step involves getting to know the particular veterinarian and his or her staff. An initial appointment can reveal much about the clinic and the people who work there.

THE FIRST VET VISIT

On your first visit, be observant of how well organized and professional the staff appears to be, how clean the examining rooms are, and how pets and their owners are treated. First impressions mean a lot! The veterinarian should be willing to take the time to address any questions you have about your dog's health without rushing to get to the next client. Does she explain medical terminology in terms you can understand? Does she appear sympathetic and knowledgeable? Does she handle your dog with patience and understanding?

An initial veterinary visit should include a thorough physical examination, which can reveal much about your dog's health. Unfortunately, a physical exam cannot detect internal parasites, which is why your veterinarian should also recommend a blood test and fecal test to check for heartworm and intestinal worms.

The first vet visit is a good time to update any vaccinations your Doberman may need and to get him microchipped if this has not already been done. Although all of these procedures—examination, tests for internal parasites, vaccinations, and microchipping—can add up to a considerable initial cost, it is always less expensive to have them done during the same visit because subsequent visits will involve additional office charges or examination fees.

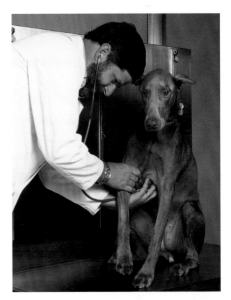

Annual veterinary checkups are necessary if you want your dog to stay healthy.

VACCINATIONS

Vaccinations can prevent a number of serious diseases, and they are absolutely necessary if you want to keep your dog in good health. A number of diseases can be fatal or result in permanent damage to tissues, while others are less threatening but are still a source of concern. Some vaccines, called core vaccines, are crucial to the health and welfare of all dogs. Other vaccines are considered noncore vaccines and are recommended at the discretion of your veterinarian. The necessity of noncore vaccines is often determined by the risks of contagion specific to the area in which you live, or the activities in which you and your dog partake. Diseases transmitted by mosquitoes or ticks, for instance, wouldn't be much of a concern if you reside in areas where these pests are not a problem.

The following are diseases your dog might be vaccinated against. Check with your veterinarian to determine which are the core vaccines for your area.

Canine Adenovirus-2

Canine adenovirus-2 is a virus that causes upper respiratory infections and results in a dry, hacking cough. It is not considered serious, but it is highly contagious and can cause problems for older dogs or dogs with compromised immune systems. Often seen in combination with other viruses, it is a common contributor to the condition called kennel cough.

Canine Coronavirus

Canine coronavirus is a gastrointestinal disease spread by direct contact with an infected dog's feces. The most common symptoms are diarrhea and vomiting, which in turn can result in dehydration that can seriously compromise the health of puppies. Symptoms are treated with intravenous fluids for dehydration and medications to control diarrhea and vomiting.

Canine Distemper

Canine distemper is considered the greatest disease threat to dogs because it is widespread and its effects can be devastating. It is fatal to the majority of puppies and half the adult dogs it ravages. Canine distemper is spread through the air as well as through contact with an infected dog's bodily secretions, urine, or feces. Symptoms include discharge from the eyes and nose, coughing, congestion, vomiting, fever, and diarrhea. It eventually affects the nervous system and can cause seizures and paralysis. There is no cure, but medications can help relieve the symptoms of vomiting, diarrhea, and seizures.

Giardia

Giardia is a protozoan parasite that infects the intestines of animals and can cause diarrhea and weight loss. This tiny bug is found in contaminated water sources such as puddles, ponds, streams, and lakes. It infects dogs who drink the contaminated water or even lick their feet after walking through it. The parasites are passed back into the environment through infected feces. Some dogs contract the disease and show few symptoms, but older dogs and puppies are at a higher risk of developing problems. A vaccine is now available to prevent giardia infection.

Infectious Canine Hepatitis (Canine Adenovirus-1)

Infectious canine hepatitis is a virus that specifically targets a dog's liver and kidneys, with the effects ranging anywhere from very mild symptoms of lethargy and fever to severe symptoms of internal bleeding and shock. Severe cases may result in death. It is

The Annual Exam

Annual physical veterinary exams should be an integral part of your pet-care routine, one reason being that your vet may notice slight changes in your dog's health that have escaped your attention.

spread through contact with an infected dog's bodily secretions, urine, or feces. The canine adenovirus-2 vaccine provides protection against this virus. Treatment consists of intravenous fluids to help combat dehydration, and diet supplements may be prescribed to minimize the disease's effect on the liver.

Kennel Cough

Kennel cough is characterized by inflammation of the trachea, bronchial tubes, and larynx, which results in a dry, nonproductive cough. It is a highly contagious respiratory disease that is caused by a number of airborne viruses and bacteria working together or alone. The most common contributors to kennel cough are *Bordetella bronchiseptica* bacteria and the canine adenovirus-2 and canine parainfluenza viruses. Even though symptoms are not severe, it is still a concern where a large number of dogs are kept, such as boarding kennels, shelters, dog shows, and training facilities. The kennel cough vaccine is administered as a nasal spray or as an injection and protects against all three of the main contributing agents. Treatment is usually limited to prescription or nonprescription cough suppressants.

Leptospirosis

Leptospirosis is a bacterial infection spread through contact with the urine of infected dogs or wild animals. This infection attacks a dog's kidneys and liver, and it can produce symptoms of fever, listlessness, vomiting, and jaundice. Several strains of bacteria are responsible for producing leptospirosis in dogs, and the prevalence of these bacteria varies in different geographic locations. The effect of vaccines is limited to lessening the severity of the disease, not preventing it, so vaccination is usually done only on the recommendation of your veterinarian. Treatment consists of antibiotic therapy.

Vaccinations help protect a dog against disease.

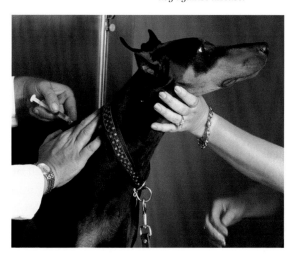

Lyme Disease

Lyme disease is a bacterial disease that can result in symptoms of listlessness, fever, loss of appetite, lameness, and arthritis. Ticks harboring *Borrelia burgdorferi* bacteria are responsible for spreading this disease, so it is a concern in areas where ticks are known to live, such as wooded or tall-grass areas. The vaccine is only necessary, therefore, for dogs exposed to such areas. This disease normally responds to antibiotic treatment.

Parainfluenza

Parainfluenza is a respiratory infection spread through contact with bodily secretions or airborne particles. It is generally a mild disease that causes symptoms of nasal discharge and coughing, but it can become serious if complicated by the onset of pneumonia. Treatment is not necessary except in the case of a secondary pneumonia infection, in which case antibiotics will be prescribed.

Parvovirus

Parvovirus is a highly contagious intestinal virus that can overwhelm a dog in a short period of time. Death often results within 2 to 3 days after the onset of symptoms. It is spread through contact with the feces of infected dogs and causes symptoms of listlessness, loss of appetite, fever, vomiting, and diarrhea. It is a particular concern for Dobermans because they (for reasons yet unknown) appear to be at a higher risk of contracting parvo than other breeds. As there is no cure, treatment is limited to supportive care such as intravenous fluids and antivomiting medications. Even with successful treatment, dogs affected by parvo may experience residual heart problems.

Rabies

Rabies is one of the most feared diseases in the world because it is readily transmittable to humans, its symptoms are horrifying, and it is almost always fatal. Very few people have been documented to survive rabies after symptoms have been presented. The symptoms are very much the same for humans and animals—increased salivation, inability to swallow, aversion to water, and delirium—all a result of the disease's assault on the nervous system. It is usually spread through the bite of an infected animal. Fortunately, through regulated use of rabies vaccines for domestic animals, the incidence of humans contracting the disease is now quite low. Check the laws in your state or municipality to find out if

Vaccination Guidelines

The following is a suggested guideline; your veterinarian may recommend a variation of this protocol.

Vaccines	Age of Puppy				Boosters
	8 wks	12wks	16wks	1yr	thereafter
Distemper years	X	X		X	every 3
Parvovirus	X	X	X	X	every 3 years
Parainfluenza	X	X		X	every 3 years
Coronavirus*	X	X		X	every 3 years
Canine adenovirus-2	X	X		X	every 3 years
Leptospirosis*	X	X		X	every 3 years
Bordetella*		X		X	as needed
Lyme disease*		X	X	X	seasonally
Giardia*	X	X		X	annually
Rabies+		X		X	every 1 to 3 years as required by law

* Optional vaccines, depending on location and risk.

+ Required by law.

a one-year or three-year rabies vaccination is required for your dog.

EAR CROPPING

Doberman Pinschers have traditionally had their ears cropped. Because ear cropping surgery is a purely cosmetic procedure, it has been banned in many countries. Where it is still legal, fanciers continue to crop their dogs in the interest of preserving the Doberman's historical identity.

Some breeders have their puppies' ears cropped when they are between 6 to 10 weeks old, before they are even ready for sale. If your puppy was not cropped when you got him, you will have to decide whether or not to have the procedure done. If you plan to show your dog, cropped ears are usually the standard in countries that allow the practice. If you plan to keep your dog as a pet, you should seriously consider the risks and drawbacks of this surgery.

Advantages of Cropping

Cropped ears will definitely affect your dog's appearance and give him a sharper, cleaner image. If you were first attracted to the

Doberman Pinschers have traditionally had their ears cropped. Where it is still legal, fanciers continue to crop their dogs in the interest of preserving the breed's historical identity.

Doberman's cropped appearance, this look might be as important to you as it was to Louis Dobermann and other early fanciers of the breed. And finally, ear cropping will make your dog more easily recognizable as a purebred Doberman.

Disadvantages of Cropping

There is always a price to pay for cosmetically enhanced good looks! The cost of surgery and the extensive postoperative care that is often involved in getting the ears to stand properly may be more than you're willing to invest. Aside from the pain and discomfort ear cropping causes your dog, the risks of anesthesia and the potential for failure (when the ears don't turn out exactly as you've envisioned) are also causes for concern.

Making the Decision to Crop

The decision to crop should be made with your eyes wide open. Here are some suggestions:

- Seek out an experienced veterinarian to perform the operation. Ear cropping is not a simple procedure. It is a skill for which some veterinarians develop great expertise and others never quite seem to get the hang of. Ask your breeder or veterinarian for recommendations.
- Be sure the veterinarian explains all the potential risks associated with this procedure. The possibility of complications such as infection, reaction to anesthetic, and scarring exists. There is also no guarantee that the natural healing process won't cause tissues to shrink and kink, causing unsightly imperfections.
- Carefully consider the postoperative care involved. If you don't think you have the time or patience to keep the ears properly taped until they are set, you may end up ruining, rather than improving, your dog's appearance. Postoperative care may endure for months in order to achieve acceptable results.
- Opt for this procedure when your dog is very young, preferably under the age of 12 weeks. Young puppies usually rebound more quickly from this surgery.

- Be aware that deformities and crop failures are rarely correctable unless the problem is extremely minor.

There is more to love about the Doberman than his appearance, so if your dog is intended strictly as a pet, you might decide the less intimidating natural look is more appropriate. Uncropped Dobermans have a more approachable appearance, which can make a difference in how others (your friends, neighbors, or elderly individuals) perceive your dog.

NEUTERING AND SPAYING

If you do not plan to show or breed your dog, the best thing you can do for yourself, your dog, and your community is to have your dog neutered or spayed. This will prevent your pet from contributing to the already overwhelming problem of pet overpopulation, as well as providing many other benefits.

Sterilization surgery will make your dog unable to reproduce, and it will eliminate many sexually driven behaviors that are difficult to manage. Unaltered male dogs are more likely to develop the habit of marking territory (urinating in the home), roaming in search of a mate, or mounting inappropriate objects—or people! They also have a greater tendency to develop aggressive behaviors. Unaltered females go through a very messy and stressful heat period at least twice per year that requires vigilance to prevent accidental breeding. In a nutshell, it can be stressful and inconvenient to own an unaltered dog.

In addition to making your dog a better pet, neutering and spaying offers valuable health benefits. Altered dogs are not susceptible to problems associated with the reproductive organs. They do not face complications of pregnancy or birth, and they do not develop tumors or infections of the uterus or ovaries. Overall, altered dogs can expect to enjoy greater longevity and a better quality of life, which is what every pet owner should desire for her dog.

Castration

Castration is the technical term for neutering a male dog. This surgical procedure involves making a small incision in front of the scrotum so that the testicles can be removed. The incision is usually closed with absorbable sutures so that postoperative care is minimal. The entire procedure takes only a few minutes and

is performed under general anesthesia so that your dog has no awareness or sensation of pain.

Castration is not considered major surgery since it does not involve entering the abdominal cavity, and recovery is usually very rapid. Your dog may be somewhat lethargic the day after surgery due to the effects of anesthesia, but he will probably be bouncing boisterously in typical Doberman style within a couple of days. Even so, veterinarians recommend limiting your dog's physical activity for at least a week after the surgery.

Ovariohysterectomy

Ovariohysterectomy is the spaying of a female dog. This procedure is more complex than castration due to the female's different anatomy, but recuperation is still quite rapid. Considered major surgery, ovariohysterectomy is performed by entering the abdominal cavity through an incision in the belly and removing the female reproductive organs. As with castration, general anesthesia prevents your dog from feeling any pain or discomfort during this procedure, and sutures are used to close the incision and minimize postoperative care.

Other than keeping the incision area clean and watching for any redness, discharge, or swelling, there is little postoperative care involved. Some veterinarians may prescribe pain medication to be administered for a day or two after surgery.

Risks of Anesthesia

Castrations and ovariohysterectomies are performed with such frequency that they are considered routine surgical procedures with very low incidence of complications. However, any surgical procedure requiring the use of anesthesia poses some risks, especially for dogs who may have preexisting conditions undetectable by physical examination. For this reason, many veterinarians recommend a blood test prior to any surgical procedure to rule out the existence of issues that may cause complications. Although optional, blood tests can give you peace of mind that your dog is healthy enough to undergo these procedures.

BREEDING

Puppies, puppies, puppies! They're cute, playful, and entertaining. Wouldn't it be fun and exciting to raise a few? If the prospect of breeding your dog seems like a rewarding and profitable idea, some important considerations might bring you back down to earth. In addition to the drawbacks and responsibilities of owning an unaltered dog, there are health concerns, veterinary expenses, and a serious commitment of time involved.

The household mess attributed to a female dog's heat cycle isn't nearly as messy as a litter of puppies can be. The prospect of raising puppies is always more appealing in theory than in reality. Puppies require a lot of care and attention for at least eight to ten weeks, until they are old enough to go to new homes. Unless you are extraordinarily vigilant in keeping the puppies' area clean, you cannot expect to do this without experiencing some odor in the house. The puppies must be handled and socialized as much as possible, and they should receive at least one series of puppy vaccinations before they are ready for sale. The cost of health care can add up to a considerable amount, depending on the number of puppies in the litter.

Health risks for the female also should not be taken lightly. Birthing is a complicated process that doesn't always follow nature's blueprint. Unexpected veterinary expenses, in addition to the high cost of meeting the health needs of the puppies, may be incurred. For these reasons, breeding has very little value as a source of financial profit and is usually reserved for those who

The decision to breed your Doberman should not be taken lightly. Breeding is a serious undertaking that requires extensive expertise, time, and money.

- ***Allowing your female Doberman to go through at least one heat cycle is good for her health or temperament.*** On the contrary, even one heat cycle puts your dog at a higher risk of developing mammary tumors. Spaying does *not* affect your dog's personality, although it *will* reduce or eliminate undesirable sexual behaviors.

- ***Allowing your female Doberman to have at least one litter of puppies prior to spaying is good for her health or temperament.*** In reality, there are no health or temperament benefits in allowing your dog to reproduce. Instead, her health risks are greatly compounded.

- ***Castrating your male Doberman will take away his "maleness."*** Although castration reduces the tendency toward aggression and helps eliminate sexual behaviors that are difficult to manage, your neutered male will still be just as bold and fearless as his genetics have programmed him to be.

have a serious interest in producing quality dogs as a labor of love.

If you plan to show your dog and have a passion to produce superior Dobermans, by all means, do your research and your best for the benefit of the breed. But if you are only looking for fun and profit, you are better off finding another hobby. There are already enough Dobermans in shelters and rescues across the country who are by-products of irresponsible breeding endeavors.

EXTERNAL PARASITES

Parasites live on or in the body of animals and obtain at least a portion of their sustenance from their hosts without providing any benefits in return. They can seriously compromise the health of dogs, especially in the case of puppies, who do not have the bodily reserves to counteract the detrimental effects of parasites.

Parasite control is not only necessary for the health of your dog, it is also important for you and your family because some parasites are easily transmitted to humans. Prevention and prompt treatment for infestations can keep your entire household healthy.

External parasites are those that live on the surface of their host, clinging to hair, crawling on skin, or burrowing into the skin. They are the most common cause of skin irritations for pets, and they are a great source of distress for both pets and their owners.

Fleas

Fleas are tiny brown insects that live on the skin of their hosts and subsist on the blood they draw from biting. One of the most common and widespread of parasitic pests, fleas can reproduce year-round in warmer climates, and they can even manage to survive colder climates when homes and doghouses provide enough warmth. Although they prefer to target dogs and cats, they have been known to bite people as well. These little creatures can definitely give you a case of the creepy-crawlies!

Symptoms of Flea Infestation

Symptoms of flea infestation include scratching; biting; the appearance of small, reddish-brown insects on your dog's fur or skin; and tiny black droppings—called flea dirt—left in your dog's coat. Besides the potential for skin and coat damage caused by scratching, fleas can cause a number of health problems. If your dog is sensitive to flea saliva, he can develop a severe allergic reaction. Puppies, due to their small size and limited blood volume, are at risk of life-threatening anemia from the loss of blood caused by flea bites. In addition, fleas are notorious for transmitting tapeworms, which can also impact your dog's health.

Eradicating Fleas

Treating a flea problem involves eliminating the fleas on your dog as well as from other places they reside in your home and yard, such as carpeting, furniture, dog beds, and outdoor areas where your dog spends time. It also involves more than one treatment for your dog and his environment because fleas in the pupae stage are impervious to pesticides. The pupae can only be treated after they have developed into adults.

There are dozens of products on the market designed to remove fleas from your pets, home, and yard. They come in a variety of forms—shampoos, dips, sprays, powders, and foggers—but the following general tips and guidelines apply to the use of any of these products:

- Vacuum carpets and wash any bedding or other fabrics prior to applying chemical flea controls. This will help to remove as many fleas and eggs as possible from the environment prior to treatment.

Flea Facts

- A female flea lays about 15 to 20 eggs per day and 600 or more eggs in her lifetime.
- The flea life cycle includes four stages of development: egg, larva, pupa, and adult.
- Fleas thrive in temperatures of 65 to 80°F (18 to 29°C) and prefer humidity levels of 75 to 85 percent.
- Fleas live an average of two to three months, but can live up to one year.
- Female fleas consume 15 times their body weight in blood daily.
- A flea can jump up to 150 times its body length.
- A typical flea population consists of 50 percent eggs, 35 percent larvae, 10 percent pupae, and 5 percent adults.

- Always follow the directions for flea control products carefully. Be especially mindful of warnings concerning the use of more than one type of product at the same time.
- All the pets in your household must be treated at the same time.
- Re-treat pets and the environment according to the timetable provided in the product instructions.

If you are unable to bring a flea infestation under control with the use of commercially available products, some products available through veterinary prescription may be more effective. You also have the option of hiring an exterminator if your property is particularly difficult to treat yourself.

Flea Prevention

Once the fleas have been removed, reinfestation can be prevented with the use of a number of products designed as repellents. Under the supervision of your veterinarian, flea collars, spot-on treatments, monthly tablets, or oral liquid treatments available at most pet supply stores or through prescription can be used. Other methods of prevention include keeping indoor environments clean by vacuuming frequently and washing pet bedding regularly. Outdoor environments can be made less conducive to harboring fleas by keeping your lawn trimmed short.

Mites

Mites are microscopic parasites that live on or in the skin of animals and can cause itching, hair loss, or skin lesions. Mites can be very damaging, and some are highly contagious. When a demodex or sarcoptic mite infection covers a large portion of a dog's body, it is considered a generalized condition and can be extremely challenging to treat. Therefore, prompt diagnosis and treatment is important for a good prognosis.

Demodex Mites

Demodex mites are commonly found on the skin of dogs. A dog's immune system efficiently keeps demodex mite populations in check so that they do not cause problems, but there are occasions when demodex mites overpopulate. When this occurs, itching, patchy hair loss, or skin lesions (usually affecting the head or legs) may develop. This condition is called demodectic mange. The skin may become inflamed and red, which is why it is also commonly referred to as red mange.

Demodectic mange tends to affect dogs with immature or weak immune systems. Dogs under the age of two, or aged dogs, are at the highest risk of developing problems. In the case of young dogs, an underdeveloped immunity (which is believed to be hereditary) is responsible for outbreaks. These dogs will usually develop a stronger immunity as they mature. Older dogs, on the other hand, may suffer from an immune-suppressing health condition that must be addressed before treatment will be successful.

A microscopic examination of skin scrapings will usually reveal if demodex mites are present. If so, your veterinarian will recommend a treatment regimen that may include several applications of prescription dips or sprays and diet supplementation to improve your dog's skin health.

Sarcoptic Mites

Sarcoptic mites produce the condition known as mange, or scabies, which is characterized by itching, hair loss, and skin lesions, in addition to the sores and scabs caused by scratching and rubbing. Because the symptoms are similar to an allergic skin reaction, veterinary diagnosis is necessary to determine if mites are responsible.

Like demodex mites, sarcoptic mites are detected by microscopic examination of skin scrapings and are treated with similar methods. Because sarcoptic mites are extremely contagious, however, other dogs in your household should be examined for possible infection as well.

Ear Mites

Ear mites tend to be a more common problem for cats than dogs, but in households where cats and dogs cohabitate, there is a good chance for infection of both species. These mites are easily transmitted by physical contact and usually take up residence in the ears of their hosts. There, they live in a protected environment where they can feed on earwax and skin oils.

Signs of ear mite infection include a dark discharge from your dog's ears, sometimes accompanied by head shaking or ear scratching. Because these signs can also be symptoms of an ear infection, veterinary diagnosis is necessary to accurately pinpoint the cause. A severe case of ear mite infection may also lead to inflammation or secondary bacterial infections.

A number of over-the-counter topical treatments are available to eradicate ear mites, but because these mites are very difficult to see with the naked eye and there are many reasons why a pet might have itchy ears with a discharge, it is best to have your veterinarian look into the ears with a magnifying otoscope to determine the exact cause and best treatment.

Ticks

Ticks are small, blood-sucking insects that live in wooded and grassy areas throughout North America. There are several species of ticks, all of which have flat, spider-like bodies and tiny heads that burrow into the skin of their hosts. On dogs, they prefer the thinner skin of the ears, head, and neck, where they often remain undetected until their bodies become so engorged with blood they can easily be seen or felt through the fur.

Keeping Ticks Out of Your Yard

To keep ticks out of your yard, keep the grass mowed so it's less suitable for them to survive, stack firewood off the ground and away from the house, and use tick-killing pesticides.

Ticks are known to transmit a number of diseases to both dogs and humans, which makes it imperative that you prevent tick bites and remove ticks immediately when they are found. It can take several hours to a couple of days for a tick to transmit a disease, so the sooner you remove a tick, the better the chance that your dog has not been infected.

Preventing Tick-Borne Diseases

If your dog is at risk of exposure, a vaccination can help prevent tick-borne diseases such as Lyme disease. Examine him for ticks immediately after he has been exposed to any environment that harbors them. If you live in an area where ticks are prevalent, keep your grass mowed to make your yard less suitable for them to survive. Tick-killing pesticides can also help keep your yard and home clear of these parasites. Many products designed for flea control will also repel ticks, including insecticide collars and spot-on treatments.

Removing a Tick

Removing a tick is as simple as grasping it close to the head with tweezers and gently pulling it off. Afterward, clean your hands, tweezers, and the bite site with disinfectant. Other methods of removal, such as dousing the tick with kerosene, are not recommended. They are not only ineffective, but they can also be harmful. If your dog displays any disease symptoms after a tick bite, seek veterinary attention immediately.

External parasites can make your Doberman uncomfortable and potentially sick. Always check your dog for fleas, mites, and ticks after he's been playing outdoors.

INTERNAL PARASITES

Internal parasites are small organisms that live inside a dog's body, specifically within the circulatory and digestive systems. Within this warm and protected environment, they feed, grow, and eventually produce eggs or larvae that leave the dog's body to infect other hosts. Controlling internal parasites is a priority because they can overburden a dog's body and cause severe symptoms or even death.

Heartworms

Heartworms are a deadly parasite that can infect the circulatory system and damage internal organs. Your dog can get heartworms after being bitten by a mosquito that has ingested the blood of another infected animal. The infective larvae (young worms), called microfilariae, circulate through his bloodstream and migrate to his heart, where they become adult worms that can grow up to 12 inches (30 cm) long. The adult worms then begin to produce a new generation of microfilariae that reenter your dog's bloodstream, beginning their life cycle all over again.

Heartworms target the right side of the heart and the blood vessels leading from the heart to the lungs. It may take months

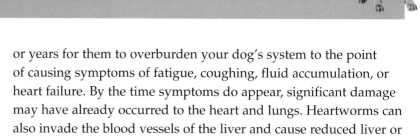

The Heartbreaking Facts About Heartworms

- Indications are that 100 percent of dogs exposed to infective heartworm larvae become ill.
- The American Heartworm Society (AHS) estimates that only 55 percent of dogs in the United States are currently on heartworm preventive, which leaves approximately 27 million dogs unprotected.
- Heartworm infection is fatal to dogs who do not receive treatment.
- By the time a dog displays symptoms of heartworm infection, permanent damage to the heart, lungs, liver, or kidneys may have already occurred.

or years for them to overburden your dog's system to the point of causing symptoms of fatigue, coughing, fluid accumulation, or heart failure. By the time symptoms do appear, significant damage may have already occurred to the heart and lungs. Heartworms can also invade the blood vessels of the liver and cause reduced liver or kidney function.

A blood test or X-ray can confirm the diagnosis of heartworm infection, and treatment will consist of killing the heartworms with poison and letting your dog's body naturally absorb the dead worms. Unfortunately, treatment can be lengthy and risky if your dog has a large infestation. Permanent damage to internal organs can further complicate recovery.

The bad news is that heartworm infection is fatal for untreated dogs. The good news is that it is completely preventable. Administering heartworm preventives should definitely be included in your health maintenance routine for your Doberman. Put it on your calendar! Daily or monthly medications are currently available, and these can be administered year-round or seasonally, depending on the risks of infection. An annual blood screening can provide additional assurance that your dog has not been infected. Research on heartworm prevention is ongoing, so check with your veterinarian to find out what kind of preventives are currently available.

Intestinal Worms

Several species of worms find that the canine digestive tract provides suitable living accommodations, including roundworms, hookworms, whipworms, and tapeworms. Some of these worms are visible to the naked eye, while others can only be detected under microscopic examination—a good reason to have your veterinarian examine a stool sample at veterinary checkups.

Roundworms

Roundworms are a common problem for puppies. These worms can grow up to 7 inches (18 cm) long and cause symptoms of lethargy, diarrhea, or vomiting. They might give your Doberman puppy a pot-bellied appearance, and their affect on his health will be evident by poor coat condition, a lack of growth, or an inability to thrive.

The effects of roundworms are not as pronounced on adult dogs, but the worms are easily passed from pregnant females to their offspring. Roundworms can become encysted in a female dog's tissues and can remain dormant until they are activated in the later stages of pregnancy during which they can infect the pups. Encysted larvae are impervious to treatment, so treating the female will not prevent transmission of these parasites to her litter. This is why *all* puppies should receive deworming treatments.

Roundworms can also be transmitted through the consumption of contaminated feces or soil, and they can infect humans. It is estimated that 5 to 20 percent of children are infected with roundworms at some point during childhood. So there are many important reasons to keep these pests under control.

You can purchase deworming treatments at pet supply stores or through your veterinarian. Like other types of parasites, migrating or encysting roundworm larvae are immune to treatment, so subsequent treatments will be necessary to kill worms that hatch later.

Hookworms

Hookworms are so named because of the barbed teeth they use to attach themselves to the wall of the intestine. They are too small to be seen by the naked eye, but their effects can be devastating for your puppy. Because hookworms survive on a diet of blood, your puppy is at risk of developing anemia, which in turn will affect his energy level and ability to thrive. Adult dogs, as well, may suffer from a lack of stamina. Other symptoms include diarrhea, weakness, and weight loss.

Like roundworms, these parasites are transmitted from female dogs to their puppies and through the consumption

of contaminated feces or soil. Hookworm larvae can also burrow directly through the skin to infect a dog. Treatments for roundworms are also effective against hookworms.

Whipworms

Whipworms are microscopic worms that have long, whip-like tails that they imbed into the wall of your dog's large intestine. These worms subsist on blood, but they do not consume as much as hookworms and do not always cause symptoms. Occasionally, their presence will be indicated by weight loss or diarrhea tinged with mucus or blood.

These worms can only be transmitted through consumption of their eggs, which are found in contaminated feces and soil. Because they do not produce as many eggs as other worm species, they can be difficult to detect through fecal examinations, and several tests may be necessary to confirm a whipworm infestation. Your veterinarian is the best source for treatment recommendations, especially because some over-the-counter dewormers are not effective against whipworms.

Tapeworms

Tapeworms are flat, segmented worms that can reach up to 6 inches (15 cm) long in your dog's small intestine. Although there are several species of tapeworms, *Dipylidium caninum* is the most common found in dogs. Fleas that ingest tapeworm eggs transmit this parasite to your dog after being consumed by him.

A heavy tapeworm infection can result in abdominal discomfort, weight loss, and vomiting, but in most cases there are few symptoms. Infection is most often detected by observing segments of the worm that are shed in your dog's stool or become stuck to the hair around your dog's anus. These body segments are actually egg casings that resemble small pieces of confetti.

Your veterinarian is your only source of treatment for tapeworms because over-the-counter dewormers are not effective against this particular parasite. You can prevent reinfestation by eliminating fleas from your dog and his environment.

Types of Intestinal Worms

The following intestinal worms can cause major problems for dogs:

- roundworms
- hookworms
- whipworms
- tapeworms
- heartworms

Some of these worms are visible to the naked eye, while others can only be detected under microscopic examination—a good reason to have your veterinarian check for them at your dog's annual veterinary checkup.

COMMON HEALTH CONCERNS

A number of health conditions are a concern for all dog owners due to their prevalence within the canine species.

Allergies

Skin and coat conditions that cause itchy skin and hair loss are common among many breeds of dog. Quite a few disorders are responsible for these symptoms, so veterinary assistance is needed to make a correct diagnosis before effective treatment can be implemented. One of the most common causes of skin conditions is allergies.

Several types of allergies can affect dogs—contact, inhalant, bacterial, food, and flea allergies—but they all have basically the same effect. Unlike humans who may react to certain allergies with respiratory symptoms or irritated eyes, canine allergies tend to affect the condition of the skin.

Puppies can be severely affected by internal parasites.

Contact Allergies

A dog may suffer an allergic reaction to a substance with which he comes into physical contact. Cleaning detergents, pesticides, or lawn chemicals are potential allergens that can cause itchy, irritated skin at the site of contact. Washing the offending substance from your dog and preventing future contact is the best way to control this type of allergy.

Inhalant Allergies

Sensitivity to pollen, mold spores, or dust mites will also result in an allergic reaction. This type of allergy is also characterized by itchy skin, but symptoms may also include head shaking, face rubbing, and feet licking. Because it is impossible to completely remove these types of allergens from your dog's environment, inhalant allergies cannot always be avoided—but they can be managed.

Your veterinarian can help you develop a management plan that may include antihistamines to relieve symptoms, shampoos to soothe itchy skin, and diet supplements to help repair and strengthen damaged skin. Allergy testing is available to isolate the source of the offending allergen so that steps can be taken to minimize your dog's exposure to it.

Just as in humans, allergies are relatively common in pets. Pesticides or lawn chemicals are potential allergens that can cause itchy, irritated skin at the site of contact.

Bacterial Allergies

Bacterial allergies develop when a dog's immune system is incapable of keeping the natural population of staph bacteria in check. The bacteria then overpopulate to cause intense itching, patchy hair loss, and skin infections called pyoderma. Managing this type of allergy may include topical or oral medications and medicated shampoo prescribed by your veterinarian. Diet supplements to help rejuvenate damaged skin are also helpful.

Food Allergies

Food allergies can have an effect on skin and coat condition by causing itchiness and excessive shedding, but they can also result in stomach upset and diarrhea. It may be challenging to determine the source of a food allergy due to the large number of ingredients in commercial dog foods, so the best course of action is to completely change your dog's diet. Some foods have grain products, which are suspected of causing food allergies in some dogs. Others have unusual protein sources such as rabbit, duck, or venison. Fortunately, there are many varieties of dog foods on the market, so it isn't too difficult to find several with completely different ingredients.

Finding an appropriate commercial dog food for the food-allergic dog is a matter of trial and error. Because the full effects of a diet change may take up to two months to show results, it may take a bit of time to find an appropriate food. Your veterinarian may also be able to provide a prescription hypoallergenic diet. But more challenging than trying to find an acceptable diet is remembering to adhere to a diet plan, which means any type of consumables you feed your dog—treats, bones, or other items—must also meet the new diet requirements.

Flea Allergies

Many dogs are sensitive to flea saliva and suffer more than the typical itchiness associated with these parasites. A flea injects its saliva into the skin when it bites, and for some dogs this causes an allergic reaction with feverish scratching that subsequently damages the skin. Secondary bacterial infections are often common, and antibiotic treatment as well as treatment to repair the damaged skin will be necessary. But the first and most important treatment for this condition is to eliminate the fleas.

Bloat (Gastric Dilatation and Volvulus)

Bloat, or gastric dilatation, refers to bloating of the stomach, a very serious condition that tends to affect deep-chested dogs such as the Doberman Pinscher. This condition can kill a dog within an hour, so become familiar with the symptoms and plan a course of action in the event that they should appear.

Bloat occurs when an excessive amount of air fills the stomach, essentially expanding it and creating intense pain. Volvulus refers to the condition that results when the bloated stomach rotates on itself, causing twists that pinch off the organ at its entry and exit points. This also shuts off blood supply to the stomach, which causes the tissues to begin dying. Without immediate emergency treatment to remove the excess air and untwist the stomach, death is imminent.

Being prepared for this emergency can mean the difference between life and death for your dog. If your veterinarian does not provide 24-hour emergency care, she should be able to provide you with a reference for a facility that does. Keep the number for your emergency provider handy.

Treatment for bloat involves removing the air in the stomach by passing a tube from the mouth to the stomach. In the case of volvulus, where twists in the stomach do not allow the passage of a tube, surgery is the only option. Dogs who have suffered bloat are at a much higher risk of developing the same condition again, so precautions should be taken to minimize this possibility. A surgical procedure

Canine Bloat

Bloat, or gastric dilatation, refers to bloating of the stomach. It occurs when an excessive amount of air fills the stomach, essentially expanding it and creating intense pain. This condition can kill a dog within an hour, so it's important to become familiar with the symptoms and plan a course of action in case they should appear.

Symptoms of Bloat

- attempts to vomit, usually unsuccessful
- difficulty defecating
- gagging
- hard, distended abdomen
- heavy drooling
- pale gums
- rapid heart rate
- rapid panting or shallow breathing
- restlessness, pacing
- signs of abdominal discomfort
- weak pulse

Preventing Bloat

- Feed smaller amounts more frequently (feed twice per day instead of once per day).
- Avoid heavy exercise 1 hour before feeding and 2 hours after feeding.
- Do not use elevated food bowls that may promote gulping air with food.
- Limit water intake immediately after feeding.
- Avoid stress and excitement at feeding time.
- Make diet changes gradually.

that involves tacking the stomach to the abdominal wall has been used successfully to prevent recurrences of volvulus.

Ear Infections

Doberman owners, breeders, veterinarians, and activists are still bickering over whether cropped Dobermans are less likely to develop ear infections than uncropped Dobermans, but the fact remains that this is a common affliction for all dogs, regardless of the type of ears they have!

An odor from the ear is usually the first noticeable sign of infection. If left untreated, additional symptoms of head shaking and scratching at the ears will develop. Physical signs of irritation such as redness, swelling, discharge, or cracked skin on the underside of the ear will show as well. Immediate veterinary attention will be necessary to successfully treat this condition as soon as any sign of infection is noticed. Antibiotics, topical ointments, and ear flushing are all treatment alternatives that may be recommended.

You can prevent ear infections by incorporating regular ear cleanings into your grooming routine. Frequent ear infections may also be the result of an underlying health condition, such as an allergy or thyroid problem. If your dog seems to have a chronic problem with ear infections, your veterinarian should investigate an underlying cause.

HERITABLE DISORDERS

The powerfully elegant physique and unwavering courage and loyalty of the Doberman Pinscher were not produced by accident. The characteristics that distinguish this breed from other breeds of dog were developed and strengthened through years of careful breeding. Establishing such consistent characteristics always entails a certain amount of inbreeding, which involves breeding closely related dogs. Although inbreeding is necessary to establish and preserve a breed type, it is also responsible for increasing the risk of heritable disorders.

Every purebred dog is known to carry genes for particular heritable disorders, and the Doberman is one breed that suffers from a fair share of genetic problems. But before you become overly concerned about hereditary health conditions, you should know that the actual incidence of heritable disorders is directly related to breeding practices.

Breeders who are careful to outcross, which is to breed their dogs to Dobermans from unrelated lines, will produce puppies less likely to inherit health problems. In addition, breeders can keep heritable problems in check by keeping meticulous health records and utilizing tests available to detect problems in their breeding stock. Thus, it is very important to scrutinize a breeder's breeding practices and analyze a dog's ancestry if you want to avoid the potential for heritable disorders.

Blood Disorders

Blood serves as a vital delivery system to nourish all the cells of the body with oxygen and nutrients. It has a built-in safety mechanism called clotting, a job performed by platelets that adhere together to plug holes in its system. Deficiencies in the platelets can prevent normal clotting and result in excessive bleeding. Both Hemophilia A and von Willebrand's disease are clotting disorders occasionally seen in the Doberman.

Hemophilia A (Factor VIII Deficiency)

Like hemophilia in humans, a recessive gene carried by females and active in males causes hemophilia A in dogs. This bleeding disorder is the result of a blood-clotting deficiency that may be mild in some cases and severe in others. Mild cases may show few if any symptoms and require no special treatments unless the dog suffers trauma or requires surgery.

More severe cases will show prolonged bleeding from any damage to blood vessels, bruising under the skin, and swelling or pain from bleeding into the joints or muscles. These cases must be managed by keeping the dog in a safe environment to prevent injuries. When excessive bleeding does occur, blood transfusions will be necessary.

Von Willebrand's Disease

Von Willebrand's disease is another blood clotting disorder that can cause abnormal bleeding. Most cases are classified as Type I, which results in a mild to moderate increase in bleeding after trauma or surgery. The more rare Types II and III can cause severe bleeding. The gene for this condition is, unfortunately, quite

Inbreeding

The characteristics that distinguish the Doberman breed from other breeds of dog were developed and strengthened through years of careful breeding. Establishing such consistent characteristics always entails a certain amount of inbreeding, which involves breeding closely related dogs. Although inbreeding is necessary to establish and preserve a breed type, it can also increase the risk of inheriting genetic defects.

widespread in the Doberman breed.

Although there is no cure, dogs with a mild form of this disease often live normal lives and show few if any symptoms. More severe cases can be managed by applying prolonged pressure to bleeding injuries and seeking veterinary assistance for cautery, sutures, or a transfusion of von Willebrand's factor.

The gene mutation that causes von Willebrand's disease has recently been discovered, giving breeders and Doberman lovers hope that the disease may eventually be eliminated from the breed. A DNA test to confirm carriers of the mutated gene is also available, so inquire about this when you purchase a dog.

Eye Diseases

Because many canine eye diseases can progress quite rapidly and result in permanent loss of vision, any eye condition should receive immediate veterinary attention.

Cataracts

Cataracts are the leading cause of blindness in dogs. A cataract begins as a small opaque spot within the lens of the eye and eventually grows to fill in the lens and cause complete blindness. The progression of the disease may occur over several months or several years.

The only cure for a cataract is surgery to replace the damaged lens with an artificial one. Fortunately, the success rate for cataract surgery is very high, even if it does tend to pinch the pocketbook. This is a very specialized surgical procedure requiring the expertise of a veterinary ophthalmologist.

Entropion

Inherited entropion involves the inward rolling of the eyelid, which causes the eyelashes to continuously irritate the eye. This problem becomes evident when there is excessive tearing, squinting, and discharge from your dog's eyes.

Surgery is the only way to correct this defect, but the success rate is high, and your dog can go on to live a happy, normal life, free from discomfort. But if you deny your dog treatment, he may eventually develop ulcers or scarring of the cornea that will permanently affect his vision. So it is best to address this problem before eye damage occurs.

Genetic Defects

Every purebred dog is known to carry genes for particular heritable disorders, and the Doberman is one breed that suffers from a fair share of genetic problems. This is because purebred dogs are often inbred to establish consistent characteristics in the breed, which increases the risk of inheriting these defects.

But before you become overly concerned about hereditary health conditions, you should know that responsible breeders keep heritable problems in check by keeping meticulous health records and utilizing tests available to detect problems in their breeding stock in order to prevent passing them on to future generations.

Progressive Retinal Atrophy

Progressive retinal atrophy (PRA) damages the retina in the eye and eventually causes total blindness. The first sign of the disease is a reduction of vision in dim light, also referred to as night blindness. As the condition worsens, the pupils in the eyes become dilated, and the lenses may become cloudy or develop cataracts. Complete blindness is inevitable, and there is, unfortunately, no cure or surgical correction available for this devastating disease.

Glandular Diseases

The glands of the endocrine system are responsible for producing hormones that affect growth, metabolism, and other bodily functions. When a gland becomes deficient in its performance, it disrupts the delicate balance that hormones maintain in the body. Although there is no cure for a failed gland, supplementation to compensate for a lack of hormones can effectively treat most problems.

Addison's Disease (Hypoadrenocorticism)

The adrenal glands produce two types of cortisone that are necessary to regulate the balance of electrolytes and to metabolize sugar, fat, and proteins in the body. When the adrenal glands fail to function, this results in the condition known as hypoadrenocorticism or Addison's disease. The most common cause of adrenal gland failure is believed to be damage from the dog's own immune system, which attacks and destroys the tissues of the gland.

This condition predominantly affects middle-aged female dogs and causes symptoms of lethargy, loss of appetite, weakness, vomiting, and diarrhea. Because these symptoms are nonspecific and may appear intermittently, it can be a challenge to diagnose, but once adrenal gland failure is suspected, the diagnosis can be confirmed by a blood test.

Treatment is fairly simple and involves replacing the missing cortisones with daily oral supplementation. An injectable medication that can be administered monthly is currently available. Treated dogs can expect to enjoy normal longevity.

Hypothyroidism

Hypothyroidism is a disorder of the thyroid gland that

commonly afflicts medium and large sized dogs, including the Doberman Pinscher. Most cases result from an auto-immune response in which the dog's own immune system attacks and destroys the tissues of the thyroid gland. As the gland is destroyed, it works harder to produce the hormones necessary to regulate metabolic rate, but it eventually becomes overwhelmed and symptoms appear.

Because hormones affect the body in so many ways, symptoms of hypothyroidism can vary greatly among individual dogs. Skin problems, hair loss, weight loss or gain, and intolerance to the cold are the most common signs of thyroid dysfunction. Blood tests, although not a foolproof way to diagnose hypothyroidism, can sometimes give an indication of abnormal hormone levels.

Administering replacement hormones in the form of twice-daily pills easily treats this condition. Although treatment must be continued for the life of the dog, the prognosis is very good for a long, healthy life.

Heart Disease

Heart disease is a condition that can affect any type of dog; it can be related to lifestyle (poor diet and lack of exercise) or develop as a consequence of other health problems. But one type of heart disease is known to affect Doberman Pinschers more often than all other breeds combined. Ongoing studies are being conducted to determine a DNA marker for dilated cardiomyopathy in the Doberman.

Dilated Cardiomyopathy

Dilated cardiomyopathy is a disease of the heart muscle that causes enlargement of the heart chambers, which in turn can result in irregular heart rhythms, heart enlargement, and, eventually, congestive heart failure. This is a very serious disorder for which sudden death is the first and only symptom for approximately 17 percent of affected dogs.

Dogs who do display prior symptoms may suffer dramatic weight loss and episodes of collapse or weakness due to irregular heart rhythms. But by the time symptoms appear, usually around middle age for most dogs, the prognosis may already be very poor. It has been shown, however, that early detection can slow the progression of the disease.

Regular physical exams can help detect irregular heart rhythms before any other signs are evident. If dilated cardiomyopathy is suspected, X-rays, ultrasounds, or electrocardiograms

Unusual changes in your dog' behavior or appearance could signal that he is ill.

may confirm the diagnosis. Treatment will vary depending on the symptoms present and the progression of the disease. Heart medications as well as diet and exercise restrictions may improve the longevity and quality of life for an affected dog.

Orthopedic Diseases

The skeletal system, which comprises bones, ligaments, tendons, muscles, and joints, is responsible for defining body shape, protecting internal organs, and facilitating mobility. When the structure of bones and joints are defective or diseased, friction or compressed nerves can cause significant pain, and reduced range of motion can diminish mobility. Bone and joint problems can be very debilitating, and care should be taken to avoid purchasing or breeding dogs with these disorders.

Hip Dysplasia

One of the most common joint problems for larger dogs is hip dysplasia, and Dobermans definitely fall into the at-risk category to inherit this disease. When the ball at the end of the femur (thigh bone) doesn't fit snugly into the socket of the hip, the leg bone moves out of place and causes friction and pain. Symptoms include rear leg lameness, skipping with the hind legs while running, and difficulty getting up, lying down, or jumping.

Hip dysplasia can appear at any age, and the severity of the condition can vary greatly among affected dogs. Milder cases

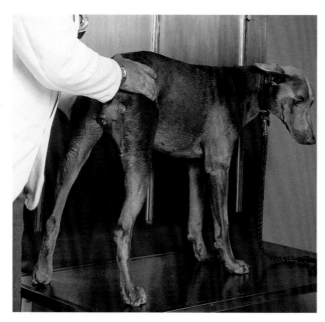

Hip and joint problems can prohibit your dog from running and playing.

may be managed with pain and anti-inflammatory medications along with exercise restrictions. Severe cases may require surgery to construct a more stable joint, or the joint may need to be replaced with an artificial one.

Because this condition is hereditary, affected dogs should not be bred. The Orthopedic Foundation for Animals (OFA) certifies dogs over the age of two years who have proven to be clear of the disease through the analysis of hip X-rays. Always ask about OFA certification for parent dogs when purchasing a puppy.

Wobbler's Syndrome (Spondylolisthesis)

Wobbler's syndrome is caused by abnormalities in the vertebrae, disks, or ligaments of the neck. The instability of the vertebrae results in spinal cord compression that causes weakness and incoordination of the limbs—thus, it gives an affected dog a wobbly appearance. The Doberman joins the Great Dane as the two breeds most commonly afflicted with this condition.

In Dobermans, symptoms often appear between three and nine years of age, and the prognosis is guarded, even for dogs who receive treatment. Wobbler's is a degenerative disease, and treatment is often limited to slowing its progression. Medical management may include restricting neck movement with a neck brace and administering anti-inflammatory medications to prevent permanent damage to the spinal cord. Surgery to stabilize the vertebrae is also an option, but it is expensive and involves the risk of severe complications.

It is obviously not advisable to breed dogs with this hereditary condition, but because symptoms do not present themselves until later in life, some dogs are bred before they are found to carry the disease. For this reason, it is important to inquire about a dog's extended family history in relation to vertebral instability before you purchase a puppy.

Skin and Pigment Disorders

Skin disorders are easily apparent on a short-coated dog like the Doberman. Hair loss, scaly skin, and skin lesions are unable to conceal themselves beneath a thin undercoat. Pigment disorders, likewise, are visibly obvious. The Doberman breed is known to suffer from a disproportionate number of both skin and pigment disorders, and dogs who have such hereditary conditions should not be bred. Most hereditary skin conditions have no cure, although they can be managed in many cases, and they may eventually be outgrown in others.

Acne

Canine acne is a skin condition that commonly affects short-coated breeds like the Doberman. Bumps and scabs appear on the chin, lips, and muzzle. These are referred to as comedones or blackheads. They are actually plugs of sebum and keratin that block the hair follicles. In severe cases, they may become infected and require antibiotic treatment, but in most cases the condition can be managed with acne products or anti-seborrheic shampoos prescribed by your veterinarian. Mild cases may not require any treatment at all.

Like human acne, symptoms tend to appear in adolescence and may continue into adulthood. Although there is no cure, the condition does not affect your dog's general health.

Behavior-Related Skin Problems

Dobermans occasionally engage in self-mutilating behaviors that have a serious impact on skin and coat condition. Acral lick dermatitis is a perplexing disorder in which the dog persistently licks a leg until the hair is lost and the skin becomes sore and weepy. In flank sucking, a dog will continuously suck at his flank until hair loss and skin damage occurs. Pododermatitis, which involves chronic foot licking, can be a symptom of an allergy or yeast infection, but it is also believed to have behavior-related roots in some instances.

The exact cause of behavior-related skin problems is not known, but the tendency to develop these behaviors is considered hereditary because they have been found to run in families. Boredom and frustration are sometimes suspected as causes because these conditions tend to surface in highly intelligent,

The Doberman breed is known to suffer from a disproportionate number of both skin and pigment disorders.

energetic dogs who are left alone for long periods of time. They may also be the result of a nervous or obsessive-compulsive disorder for which treatment is often elusive. Your veterinarian may prescribe behavior modification and antidepressant medications, as well as topical corticosteroids for skin damage.

Color Dilution Alopecia

Color dilution alopecia is a condition associated with dogs who have been bred for unusual colors. In the Doberman's case, this applies to fawn (a dilution of a red or brown), and blue (a dilution of black). It results in patchy hair loss over the light-colored areas of the body, often beginning along the back and spreading to other areas. This disorder may affect up to 90 percent of blue Dobermans and 75 percent of fawns, although the severity varies greatly.

Hair loss may initially become evident anywhere from six months to three years of age. Unfortunately, the resulting hair loss is permanent. But a dog can otherwise live a healthy life with this condition. Other occasional symptoms associated with the condition, such as scaly skin or bacterial skin infections, can be managed with moisturizing products and antibiotics.

Demodicosis

The Doberman is one of the breeds susceptible to demodicosis, a condition normally affecting dogs under the age of two. An immature or deficient immune system allows the overpopulation of demodectic mites, which cause patchy hair loss. Treatment may be necessary to control the mites, but the condition is often outgrown as the dog—and his immune system—matures.

Hypopigmentation

Hypopigmentation refers to any lack of pigment in the skin or fur. One form of hypopigmentation that affects Dobermans is restricted to a lack of pigment in the nose or lips, a condition that turns a normally dark-colored nose or lips pink. This is thought to be caused by the dog's own immune system attacking the melanin in the skin and destroying the pigment. The condition may present itself later in life, but thankfully, it is not considered harmful and treatment is not necessary.

Another form of hypopigmentation in Dobermans is albinism. It should be noted that albino Dobermans are not always completely white. Some may show light shades of pigment, freckles, or other coloring. While a few fanciers admire white Dobermans and attempt to perpetuate this condition in the breed, a lack of pigment does cause some health concerns. Albino Dobermans are known to be photosensitive (sensitive to light) and more prone to sunburn and skin cancer. It is suspected that many other health problems are linked to albinism, including abnormalities of the immune, skeletal, and neurological systems.

The effects of hypopigmentation may be more than skin deep, as it may also be responsible for undesirable personality traits or behavioral problems. Although not proven, some claim the incidence of fearfulness, learning difficulties, and aggression are higher in the albino Doberman.

It is not surprising, then, that the DPCA breed standard disqualifies albino Dobermans, and you should be hesitant about purchasing a white Doberman simply because he is unique or rare.

ALTERNATIVE HEALTH CARE

Is your dog prone to emotional extremes like anxiety or excitability? Does he suffer from a medical condition for which conventional medicine has proven ineffective? Does your dog have adverse reactions to synthetic drugs? These are just some of the situations that have been addressed with the application of alternative medicine.

Many veterinarians now specialize in the use of herbs, homeopathy, acupuncture, and chiropractic techniques in the course of administering health care to animals. And while science has yet been unable to determine exactly how or why alternative health care treatments work, their effectiveness is evident in their historical longevity and the many testimonials of those who have used them with success.

The most important consideration in choosing alternative health care for your dog is finding a qualified veterinarian. For example, members of the American Holistic Veterinary Medical Association (AHVMA) are veterinarians who practice various methods of holistic health care, and an increasing number of organizations

Benefits of Chiropractic Care

Chiropractic care can benefit dogs who suffer from musculo-skeletal problems involving the neck, back, legs, or tail. It has also been noted as a remedy for internal disorders and is used as a supplement to conventional medicine to help speed recovery.

offer veterinary training and certification in these various holistic fields.

Acupuncture

Acupuncture is an ancient Chinese treatment based on the principle of chi, which is the energy force that circulates through the bodies of all living creatures. This energy force is manipulated by inserting tiny needles into the skin at certain points where chi is known to travel through the body. These transportation routes, called meridians, correspond to various organs and tissues in the body. By manipulating the flow of chi, acupuncture influences healing at specific locations.

Acupuncture is a highly specialized holistic field. If you seek this type of treatment for your dog, investigate the websites for The International Veterinary Acupuncture Society (IVAS) at www.ivas.org and the American Academy of Veterinary Acupuncture (AAVA) at www.aava.org.

Chiropractic

Chiropractic care is becoming just as popular for pets as it is for humans! It's not just used as a treatment for health problems; it can also be incorporated into regular health maintenance routines. Signs of neuralgic dysfunction, uneven gait, unbalanced stance, or neck or back pain may indicate a need for chiropractic care. A veterinary chiropractor will physically manipulate your dog's neck, back, legs, or tail to assist healing in other parts of your dog's body.

Chiropractic is most commonly used to treat musculo-skeletal problems in dogs, but it is also used to treat internal disorders, to help speed recoveries from illness or surgery, and to compliment conventional medical treatments.

Qualified veterinarians can be found through the American Veterinary Chiropractic Association (AVCA) website at www.animalchiropractic.org.

Herbs

Herbs are plants that have been valued for centuries for their health-enhancing and medicinal qualities. They have been used to treat a wide variety of symptoms in both humans and animals, including allergies, arthritis, skin problems, urinary problems, and joint problems. They have also been touted as having a positive effect on mood, energy levels, and anxiety. The popularity of herbal remedies for pets has resulted in a proliferation of herbal supplements that are now available at many pet supply outlets.

You might be drawn to the natural quality of herbs, but just because they are derived from nature (as opposed to synthetically based) doesn't mean you can assume they are safe. Some herbs are toxic to pets, and some are known to interact with certain drugs or to cause surgical complications. This is why it is important to use herbs only at the advice of a veterinary herbalist.

The Veterinary Botanical Medicine Society (VBMA) trains and certifies veterinarians in this holistic specialty. You can seek more information or find veterinary referrals at the VBMA website at www.vbma.org.

Homeopathy

Homeopathy involves administering minute amounts of a substance that would, if given in larger doses, cause similar symptoms as the illness being treated. Like other holistic treatment methods, its mode of effectiveness is unproven, but it is possible that such treatments boost a dog's immune response to a disease.

Veterinarians who specialize in homeopathy are educated and certified by the Academy of Veterinary Homeopathy (AVH). You can find information, resources, and referrals on the AVH website at www.theavh.org.

EMERGENCIES AND FIRST AID

No matter how much effort you put into protecting your dog's health and safety, there is always the possibility of an accident—an unforeseen occurrence that can cause illness or injury to your beloved pet. If your Doberman swallowed poison, got hit by a car, or choked on an object, would you know what to do? Being prepared for an emergency can sometimes mean the difference between life and death.

Handling a Sick or Injured Animal

A sick or injured dog who is in a great deal of discomfort may be unwilling to cooperate with your attempts to help him. You should always exercise caution in handling a sick or injured

- bandage scissors
- Benadryl
- buffered aspirin
- cotton balls
- cotton swabs
- Epsom salts
- eye wash
- first aid tape
- gauze rolls
- hydrogen peroxide
- muzzle
- oral syringe
- petroleum jelly
- rectal thermometer
- rubbing alcohol
- sterile gauze pads (various sizes)
- styptic powder
- triple antibiotic ointment
- tweezers
- vet wrap bandages

animal and use methods of restraint when necessary. Methods of restraint can prevent injury to you and help immobilize your dog so he can be transported safely to a veterinary facility.

Muzzle

A muzzle can prevent your dog from biting as you attempt to assist him. You can fashion a makeshift muzzle out of a strip of cloth, rope, or your dog's leash. Tie the material around your dog's muzzle with a single knot under the jaw. Then bring each end under the ears to be tied at the base of his skull. The muzzle should be tight enough to prevent it from slipping off, but not so tight that it causes additional discomfort. Note that this form of restraint should not be used on a dog with mouth injuries or breathing problems.

Body Wrap

A body wrap can keep your dog from causing further damage to himself, as well as provide warmth if he is suffering from shock or hypothermia. If you wrap a blanket around your Doberman with his legs tucked under him (to prevent him from struggling), it will also make it easier to move him onto a stretcher for transportation.

Stretcher

When a larger dog like the Doberman is incapacitated, it can be a challenge to lift and transport him. This job is accomplished more easily with two people and a stretcher. A stretcher can be constructed from a blanket, floor mat, or a piece of plywood. After your dog is moved onto the stretcher, each person can lift an end to safely get him to a vehicle for transport to your veterinarian.

Emergency Procedures

In some situations, you must provide medical attention when your veterinarian is not immediately available. First-aid procedures can save your dog's life and increase the chance of a healthy recovery.

Bleeding

If your dog suffers an injury that results in profuse bleeding, prevent excessive loss of blood by putting a clean cloth or towel over the wound and applying pressure to it with your hand. Then

It is important to keep written instructions with your pet first aid kit to avoid wasting valuable time trying to locate this information in an emergency. The following information should be stored with your first aid supplies:

- *Emergency Contact Information:* This should include your name, address, and phone number, as well as your veterinarian's name and phone number. Any pertinent health information on your dog, such as allergies, reactions to medications, and preexisting health conditions should also be included.

- *Dosage Chart:* Consult with your veterinarian ahead of time to get dosage information for any medications kept in your first-aid kit.

- *Pet First-Aid Guide:* A simple first-aid guide can provide an invaluable reference in an emergency situation. The guide should be well organized so that information can be found quickly.

immediately transport your dog to a veterinary facility.

A tourniquet may be applied in the case of a serious wound to a limb, but this should only be done if the loss of blood is great enough to be considered life threatening. A rope or strip of cloth can be tied around the limb above the wound to cut off the blood supply to the injury. Unfortunately, this cuts off blood to the entire limb and increases the risk of possible amputation. To minimize this risk, the tourniquet should be loosened for 20 seconds every 15 minutes.

Bleeding from the nose or coughing up blood may be signs of internal bleeding. If you believe your dog has suffered internal damage, wrap him in a blanket to keep him warm, and transport him to a veterinarian immediately.

Burns

Burns can be caused by contact with a heat source, an electrical source, or a caustic chemical, but all these situations are treated similarly. In the case of a chemical burn, the area must be flushed with lots of cold water to remove as much chemical residue as possible and to cool the skin. Heat and electrical burns should also be flushed with cold water to cool the skin quickly and prevent further damage to tissues. Cold compresses should be applied on the way to the veterinarian's office (an ice pack wrapped in a towel works well for this).

Because burns do not show the full extent of damage to the

The following are common
dog-related emergencies:

- bleeding
- fractures
- shock
- burns
- choking
- cuts and abrasions
- heatstroke
- frostbite and
  hypothermia
- poisoning
- snake bites
- insect bites and stings
- seizures

skin immediately, do not wait for symptoms to worsen before treating the burn. If the skin appears mildly red, it may blossom into blisters, swelling, or sloughing of the skin later. Severe burns can easily lead to shock, so immediate veterinary attention is imperative.

Choking

If your dog is choking on an object and the object is clearly visible in his throat, attempt to remove it with your fingers, pliers, or tweezers, as long as you are not in danger of being bitten. Otherwise, assist your dog in expelling the object by placing your hands on each side of his rib cage just behind the elbows and administering several quick chest compressions. This will force the air out of his lungs, and hopefully dislodge the object.

After the object is removed, observe your dog carefully. If he shows any sign of throat swelling or injury to the throat, seek veterinary attention immediately.

Cuts and Abrasions

Minor cuts and abrasions should be cleaned thoroughly with water and treated with an antibiotic ointment. If the cut involves bleeding that does not stop, or the injury seems to have difficulty healing, have it checked by your veterinarian.

Fractures

Fractures can be very painful, so you may have to restrain your dog before handling him. If your dog is unable to walk, you will have to transport him on a stretcher. You can prevent him from struggling and causing additional injury to himself by using a body wrap. If a splint is necessary to stabilize the broken limb, roll newspaper around the limb and tape it securely. The splint should cover the joints both above and below the fracture.

Heatstroke

Heatstroke is a very serious condition caused by overheating. This can happen very easily during extremely hot weather, especially if your dog has been exerting himself without the availability of shade or fresh water to help him cool down. In addition to having an extremely high body temperature, a dog suffering from heatstroke may collapse, vomit, or have difficulty breathing. Lower his body temperature immediately by placing him in a tub of cool water, wrapping him in a cold, wet towel, or soaking him with a garden hose. Prompt veterinary attention for this potentially fatal condition is a priority.

Hypothermia and Frostbite

Hypothermia occurs when your dog's body temperature goes below normal as a result of being exposed to a cold environment. Another hazard of severely cold weather is frostbite, which damages the tissues of limbs and other extremities. You can tell if your dog has been overexposed to the cold if you see him shivering or limping, or if his skin has become red or discolored.

In the case of hypothermia, warm your dog as quickly as possible. Move him to a warm area and wrap him in a blanket. You can also use hot water bottles or hot packs (wrapped in towels) to help warm him. For frostbite, warm the affected area with a towel soaked in lukewarm water. Do not attempt to rub or massage frostbitten areas because this can damage the tissues. If your dog has suffered from hypothermia, or if frostbitten areas remain discolored or numb, seek veterinary attention.

Poisoning

Poisoning can occur any time your dog consumes a substance that is toxic to his system. Cleaning products, antifreeze, medications, and toxic foods and plants are common causes of pet poisonings. Symptoms of poisoning can include vomiting, diarrhea, loss of coordination, excessive salivation, or seizures.

Never attempt to induce vomiting without first contacting your veterinarian or calling the ASPCA Animal Poison Control Center Hotline at (888) 426-4435. If you know what substance caused the poisoning, have the product information available when you seek professional advice. It is always a good practice to keep hydrogen peroxide or syrup of ipecac on hand in case you are instructed to induce vomiting.

Seizures

Seizures occur when abnormal bursts of message impulses from the brain cause a loss of consciousness and involuntary muscle contractions. A dog in seizure may jerk, thrash, and snap, sometimes violently. It is important not to handle or attempt to

Causes of Seizures

Seizures in dogs can have a number of underlying physical causes, including hypoglycemia thyroid dysfunction, lead poisoning, brain lesions, encephalitis, diabetes, and distemper.

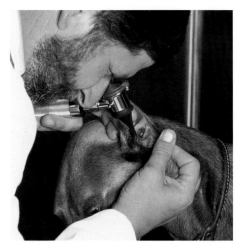

Medical emergencies require immediate veterinary care.

restrain your dog, as this may end up causing injury to you or him. You may want to move your dog away from stairs or furnishings (or place pillows and blankets around him) for his safety until the seizure has subsided. Then seek immediate veterinary attention.

Shock

Shock is the body's natural reaction to trauma or loss of blood. It causes blood pressure to drop as a defense against excessive blood loss. However, it also causes a lack of blood supply throughout the body, which can result in organ failure, unconsciousness, and even death. Signs of shock include abnormal breathing, weak pulse, dilated pupils, and a lack of responsiveness. Wrap your dog in a blanket for warmth and keep him as quiet as possible during transport to a veterinary facility.

Disaster Preparedness

Natural disasters, chemical spills, and terrorist attacks are frightening because they can occur any place at any time, sometimes without warning. If you had to flee for your life, would you be prepared? Hopefully, you have taken the advice of the Red Cross and prepared a disaster kit for your household, but did you remember to include your canine family member?

The aftermath of Hurricane Katrina's assault on the southern coast of the United States in 2005 made it clear what happens to pets who are abandoned in the wake of a disaster. Tens of thousands of animals were left to fend for themselves in dangerous conditions, causing heartbreak for their owners and resulting in massive and costly rescue operations to try to save them. If anything good came out of this experience, it is the awareness that humans are not the only victims of such disasters. It has also spurred the government and shelter operations (for both humans and animals) to make changes in how they respond to such situations.

So be sure to assemble a disaster kit for your dog, too! Make a list of kennels, shelters, and other places in your area that can provide temporary lodging for your dog, or make advance arrangements with a friend or relative to care for your dog in the event of an emergency.

THE OLDER DOG

Thanks to better diets and modern medical care, dogs are experiencing greater longevity than ever before. This is great news because you want to enjoy as many years as possible with your canine companion! But it also means you may have to deal with age-related health conditions at some point in your dog's life. If you have long enjoyed the faithful service of your Doberman, your goal should be to reward him with the best quality of life possible in his senior years. This means managing age-related conditions so that he can be comfortable and happy.

Signs of Aging

- arthritis or joint stiffness
- circulatory problems
- decreased kidney function
- dental problems
- ear infections
- lower energy level
- reduced vision or hearing
- skin or fleshy tumors
- weight loss or weight gain

Arthritis

Arthritis tends to affect most dogs to some degree as they get older. Joints begin to degenerate with age and can cause pain and soreness. If your dog shows difficulty in getting up, lying down, climbing stairs, or jumping, diet supplements may help to provide additional lubrication for stiff joints. Your veterinarian may also prescribe pain relievers or anti-inflammatories if your Doberman is experiencing significant discomfort.

Many products are available to assist arthritic dogs, including orthopedic beds, ramps, and heated blankets, but the best medicine is moderate exercise in the form of daily walks. A sedentary lifestyle aggravates arthritic conditions, so make sure your older dog gets some exercise on a regular basis.

Cancer

Cancer is a common diagnosis for older dogs, but it is not necessarily a fatal condition. Some cancers are less invasive and can be removed or treated with surgery or medications. More aggressive forms of cancer can sometimes be treated successfully if caught early. Veterinary medical advances have made more options available for the treatment of cancer in pets, including chemotherapy and radiation. But successful treatment hinges on early detection, so being observant of any symptoms of illness and seeking prompt veterinary care can mean all the difference in the world.

Dental Disease

Dental disease is a common problem for older dogs, especially for those who have not received regular dental care throughout their lives. Dental problems can be extremely painful, and loss of teeth can make eating difficult. Have your veterinarian examine your senior's teeth annually and take whatever steps are necessary to maintain his health and comfort.

Heart Disease

Thickening of the heart valves in an older dog, a condition called chronic valvular heart disease, causes abnormal blood flow that forces the heart to work harder and leads to heart enlargement and possible heart failure. Existing cardiac damage is irreparable, but its progression can often be slowed with proper medical treatment. Detecting this condition early by watching for symptoms of fatigue, and getting prompt veterinary treatment, can help prolong the life and comfort of your older dog.

Obesity

Obesity is the most common problem for older dogs. Slower metabolism and decreased energy levels may dictate that a diet change is in order. Watch your older dog closely for weight gain, measure his food carefully, and adjust his diet accordingly. Diets formulated specifically for seniors can provide fewer calories (or assist with other health conditions associated old age).

A sedentary lifestyle aggravates many health conditions, so make sure your older dog gets some exercise on a regular basis.

Reduction of Senses

It is not unusual for older dogs to lose some acuity of their senses. Eyesight may diminish due to hardening of the eye lens that naturally occurs with age. You may notice your older dog becoming less responsive to verbal commands due to a progressive loss of hearing. Older dogs can also lose some sensation of taste and become less vivacious eaters. Always have these symptoms evaluated by your veterinarian to be sure an underlying health condition, such as an ear infection or cataract, is not responsible. Although dogs tend to adapt to age-related changes quite well, you may have to make some adjustments to compensate for your dog's deficiencies.

Combining hand signals with your verbal commands will help you communicate more effectively with a hearing-impaired dog. To prevent a sight-impaired dog from bumping into things, keep him leashed in unfamiliar environments and avoid rearranging furniture. Change to a more palatable diet if your dog has lost taste sensation; this will encourage better eating and prevent weight loss.

Urinary Problems

Urinary problems are common in older dogs, but that doesn't mean you have to accept urine dribbling and household accidents as inevitable signs of aging. There are a number of causes for these problems, so a veterinary examination should be performed to detect a possible underlying health condition. If urinary problems are indeed the result of reduced liver and kidney function, special diets and medications can help minimize them.

Older dogs can also suffer from decreased production of the hormones necessary to maintain sphincter muscle tone, which results in the dribbling of urine. This problem may benefit from hormone therapy prescribed by your veterinarian. In either case, you may also need to invest in a dog bed that can be easily cleaned, and be prepared to take your dog out more frequently to prevent accidents.

SAYING GOOD-BYE

The greatest emotional hardship in owning a dog is eventually having to say good-bye. It doesn't seem fair that dogs do not live as long as humans, but this is a fact of life with which we are unfortunately burdened. And as much as we hope and pray our

dogs will leave this world quietly and peacefully in their sleep, reality rarely plays out this way. We are usually left with the heart-wrenching decision to ease our dog's transition into death in order to prevent unnecessary suffering and pain.

What is Euthanasia?

Euthanasia is a term that means good death. Veterinarians and humane organizations are equipped to euthanize animals by administering an overdose of anesthetic via intravenous injection. This drug shuts down nerve impulses, causes brain activity to cease, and relaxes muscles until the heart and lungs stop functioning. Death follows very quickly, usually within a few seconds, without any pain or discomfort felt by the animal.

Making the Decision to Euthanize

The decision to euthanize a dog is extremely personal. There are many factors that go into making this decision, including economics, the age of the dog, his quality of life, and the short-term recuperation and long-term prognosis of any health condition. In the end, you are left to consider what is best for your dog because this is the most important consideration if you truly love your pet. Prolonging your dog's suffering in order to avoid your own pain of loss is never the right thing to do.

Interment or Cremation

When your dog has been released from life, you will need to decide how to treat the remains. Some people find a sense of closure by taking care of this duty themselves, preferring to bury their pet on their own property, but care should be taken to comply with any local ordinances. Established pet cemeteries also offer a place to inter your pet.

The business or organization that euthanizes your dog may offer the option of cremation as part of its services. You can leave the responsibility of disposing of your dog's remains in their hands, or you can choose to preserve his ashes in an urn if you like. However you decide to handle your dog's remains, it should be done in a way that will not leave you with feelings of guilt or regret. You have done the best thing for your dog, even if it hurts you tremendously, and you do not need the extra emotional baggage of contrition.

Hospice Care

If your dog is terminally ill but you're not ready to let go, you may want to look into home hospice care. Some veterinary hospitals and organizations now offer this service, which keeps the animals comfortable in their own homes and gives family members time to come to terms with their impending loss. If you are interested in learning more about veterinary hospice care, ask your vet or contact your closest veterinary school. The American Association of Human-Animal Bond Veterinarians (AAH-ABV) offers information on home hospice care on their website at http://aah-abv.org.

Coping With the Loss

Coping with the death of a pet is complicated by social and religious stigmas that place little significance on the death of animals. But those who have been through the loss of a pet know how excruciatingly painful and traumatic it can be. So seek out others who have experienced the

Your dog's overall quality of life should be the first and most important factor you consider as he advances in age.

same kind of loss because they are more likely to be sympathetic, understanding, and emotionally supportive. If you are having exceptional difficulty letting go of the pain and find yourself suffering from the physical and psychological effects of depression, do not hesitate to seek professional counseling from a grief counselor or clergyman.

It is more important to deal with your grief in ways that help you find closure rather than attempting to meet the expectations of others. In other words, heal your grief in your own way and do not be too concerned about what others think. Memorials in the form of a photo plaque, planting a tree, or donating to an animal welfare organization are great ways to remember your dog.

Time does heal all pain, even if it doesn't seem like it when you're at the height of grief. There will always be a special place reserved in your heart for the precious Doberman you lost, but this is not something to be ignored or avoided; it is what keeps your legacy of love alive.

Even with your best efforts to give your dog a long and healthy life, there are no guarantees that health issues won't present themselves at times. But when you do everything with the best interest of your dog in mind, you are worthy of the love and devotion your Doberman bestows on you so selflessly and unconditionally. So enjoy every moment with your Doberman! The memories you make together will last a lifetime.

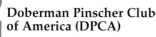

ASSOCIATIONS AND ORGANIZATIONS

DOBERMAN PINSCHER CLUBS

Doberman Pinscher Club of America (DPCA)
9821 Dunbar Lane
El Cajon, CA 92021-2623
www.dpca.org

Doberman Pinscher Club of Canada (DPCC)
1140 Rock Street
Victoria, BC V8P 2B8
Canada
Telephone: (250) 995-1675
www.dpcc.ca

The Dobermann Club United Kingdom
Telephone: 01205 821583
info@thedobermannclub.co.uk

United Doberman Club (UDC)
P.O. Box 58455
Renton, WA 98058-1455
www.uniteddobermanclub.com

BREED CLUBS

American Kennel Club (AKC)
5580 Centerview Drive
Raleigh, NC 27606
Telephone: (919) 233-9767
Fax: (919) 233-3627
E-mail: info@akc.org
www.akc.org

Canadian Kennel Club (CKC)
89 Skyway Avenue,
Suite 100
Etobicoke, Ontario
M9W 6R4
Canada
Telephone: (416) 675-5511
Fax: (416) 675-6506
E-mail: information@ckc.ca
www.ckc.ca

Federation Cynologique Internationale (FCI)
Secretariat General de la FCI
Place Albert 1er, 13
B – 6530 Thuin
Belqique
www.fci.be

The Kennel Club
1 Clarges Street
London
W1J 8AB
England
Telephone: 0870 606 6750
Fax: 0207 518 1058
www.the-kennel-club.org.uk

United Kennel Club (UKC)
100 E. Kilgore Road
Kalamazoo, MI 49002-5584
Telephone: (269) 343-9020
Fax: (269) 343-7037
E-mail: pbickell@ukcdogs.com
www.ukcdogs.com

PET SITTERS

National Association of Professional Pet Sitters
15000 Commerce Parkway
Suite C
Mt. Laurel, New Jersey 08054
Telephone: (856) 439-0324
Fax: (856) 439-0525
E-mail: napps@ahint.com
www.petsitters.org

Pet Sitters International
201 East King Street
King, NC 27021-9161
Telephone: (336) 983-9222
Fax: (336) 983-5266
E-mail: info@petsit.com
www.petsit.com

RESCUE ORGANIZATIONS AND ANIMAL WELFARE GROUPS

American Humane Association (AHA)
63 Inverness Drive East
Englewood, CO 80112
Telephone: (303) 792-9900
Fax: (303) 792-5333
www.americanhumane.org

American Society for the Prevention of Cruelty to Animals (ASPCA)
424 E. 92nd Street
New York, NY 10128-6804
Telephone: (212) 876-7700
www.aspca.org

Royal Society for the Prevention of Cruelty to Animals (RSPCA)

Telephone: 0870 3335 999

Fax: 0870 7530 284

www.rspca.org.uk

The Humane Society of the United States (HSUS)

2100 L Street, NW

Washington, DC 20037

Telephone: (202) 452-1100

www.hsus.org

SPORTS

Canine Freestyle Federation, Inc.

Secretary: Brandy Clymire

E-mail: secretary@canine-freestyle.org

www.canine-freestyle.org

International Agility Link (IAL)

Global Administrator:

Steve Drinkwater

E-mail: yunde@powerup.au

www.agilityclick.com

North American Dog Agility Council

11522 South Hwy 3

Cataldo, ID 83810

www.nadac.com

North American Flyball Association

www.flyball.org

1400 West Devon Avenue #512

Chicago, IL 6066

Telephone: (800) 318-6312

United States Dog Agility Association

P.O. Box 850955

Richardson, TX 75085-0955

Telephone: (972) 487-2200

www.usdaa.com

World Canine Freestyle Organization

P.O. Box 350122

Brooklyn, NY 11235-2525

Telephone: (718) 332-8336

www.worldcaninefreestyle.org

THERAPY

Delta Society

875 124th Ave NE, Suite 101

Bellevue, WA 98005

Telephone: (425) 226-7357

Fax: (425) 235-1076

E-mail: info@deltasociety.org

www.deltasociety.org

Therapy Dogs Incorporated

P.O. Box 5868

Cheyenne, WY 82003

Telephone: (877) 843-7364

E-mail: therdog@sisna.com

www.therapydogs.com

Therapy Dogs International (TDI)

88 Bartley Road

Flanders, NJ 07836

Telephone: (973) 252-9800

Fax: (973) 252-7171

E-mail: tdi@gti.net

www.tdi-dog.org

TRAINING

Animal Behavior Society

www.animalbehavior.org

Association of Pet Dog Trainers (APDT)

150 Executive Center Drive

Box 35

Greenville, SC 29615

Telephone: (800) PET-DOGS

Fax: (864) 331-0767

E-mail: information@apdt.com

www.apdt.com

National Association of Dog Obedience Instructors (NADOI)

PMB 369

729 Grapevine Hwy.

Hurst, TX 76054-2085

www.nadoi.org

VETERINARY AND HEALTH RESOURCES

Academy of Veterinary Homeopathy (AVH)

P.O. Box 9280

Wilmington, DE 19809

Telephone: (866) 652-1590

Fax: (866) 652-1590

E-mail: office@TheAVH.org

www.theavh.org

American Academy of Veterinary Acupuncture (AAVA)

100 Roscommon Drive
Suite 320
Middletown, CT 06457
Telephone: (860) 635-6300
Fax: (860) 635-6400
E-mail: office@aava.org
www.aava.org

American Animal Hospital Association (AAHA)

P.O. Box 150899
Denver, CO 80215-0899
Telephone: (303) 986-2800
Fax: (303) 986-1700
E-mail: info@aahanet.org
www.aahanet.org/index.cfm

American College of Veterinary Internal Medicine (ACVIM)

1997 Wadsworth Blvd.
Suite A
Lakewood, CO 80214-5293
Telephone: (800) 245-9081
Fax: (303) 231-0880
Email: ACVIM@ACVIM.org
www.acvim.org

American College of Veterinary Ophthalmologists (ACVO)

P.O. Box 1311
Meridian, Idaho 83860
Telephone: (208) 466-7624
Fax: (208) 466-7693
E-mail: office@acvo.com
www.acvo.com

American Holistic Veterinary Medical Association (AHVMA)

2218 Old Emmorton Road
Bel Air, MD 21015
Telephone: (410) 569-0795
Fax: (410) 569-2346
E-mail: office@ahvma.org
www.ahvma.org

American Veterinary Medical Association (AVMA)

1931 North Meacham Road
Suite 100
Schaumburg, IL 60173
Telephone: (847) 925-8070
Fax: (847) 925-1329
E-mail: avmainfo@avma.org
www.avma.org

ASPCA Animal Poison Control Center

1717 South Philo Road
Suite 36
Urbana, IL 61802
Telephone: (888) 426-4435
www.aspca.org

British Veterinary Association (BVA)

7 Mansfield Street
London
W1G 9NQ
England
Telephone: 020 7636 6541
Fax: 020 7436 2970
E-mail: bvahq@bva.co.uk
www.bva.co.uk

Canine Eye Registration Foundation (CERF)

VMDB/CERF
1248 Lynn Hall
625 Harrison St.
Purdue University
West Lafayette, IN
47907-2026
Telephone: (765) 494-8179
E-mail: CERF@vmbd.org
www.vmdb.org

Orthopedic Foundation for Animals (OFA)

2300 NE Nifong Blvd
Columbus, Missouri
65201-3856
Telephone: (573) 442-0418
Fax: (573) 875-5073
E-mail: ofa@offa.org
www.offa.org

PUBLICATIONS

BOOKS

Goldstein, Robert S., V.M.D., and Susan J. *The Goldsteins' Wellness & Longevity Program.* Neptune City: T.F.H. Publications, 2005.

Morgan, Diane. *Good Dogkeeping.* Neptune City: T.F.H. Publications, 2005.

MAGAZINES

AKC *Family Dog*
American Kennel Club
260 Madison Avenue
New York, NY 10016
Telephone: (800) 490-5675
E-mail: familydog@akc.org
www.akc.org/pubs/
familydog

AKC *Gazette*
American Kennel Club
260 Madison Avenue
New York, NY 10016
Telephone: (800) 533-7323
E-mail: gazette@akc.org
www.akc.org/pubs/gazette

Dog & Kennel
Pet Publishing, Inc.
7-L Dundas Circle
Greensboro, NC 27407
Telephone: (336) 292-4272
Fax: (336) 292-4272
E-mail: info@petpublishing.
com
www.dogandkennel.com

Dog Fancy
Subscription Department
P.O. Box 53264
Boulder, CO 80322-3264
Telephone: (800) 365-4421
E-mail: barkback@dogfancy.
com
www.dogfancy.com

Dogs Monthly
Ascot House
High Street, Ascot,
Berkshire SL5 7JG
United Kingdom
Telephone: 0870 730 8433
Fax: 0870 730 8431
E-mail: admin@rtc-
associates.freeserve.co.uk
www.corsini.co.uk/
dogsmonthly

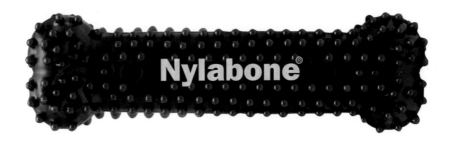

ABOUT THE AUTHOR

Janice Biniok has written numerous articles and several books on companion animals, including *The Toy and Miniature Poodle* (T.F.H. Publications, Terra Nova series, 2006). She has an English degree from the University of Wisconsin-Milwaukee and is a member of the Dog Writers Association of America, Inc. Janice lives on a small farm in Waukesha, Wisconsin, with her husband, two sons, and several four-legged members of the family.

PHOTO CREDITS